interpretations

Vol 5

by joji locatelli and veera välimäki

photographs by rafael delceggio
theme texts by jenica poduje

POM POM PRESS
LONDON

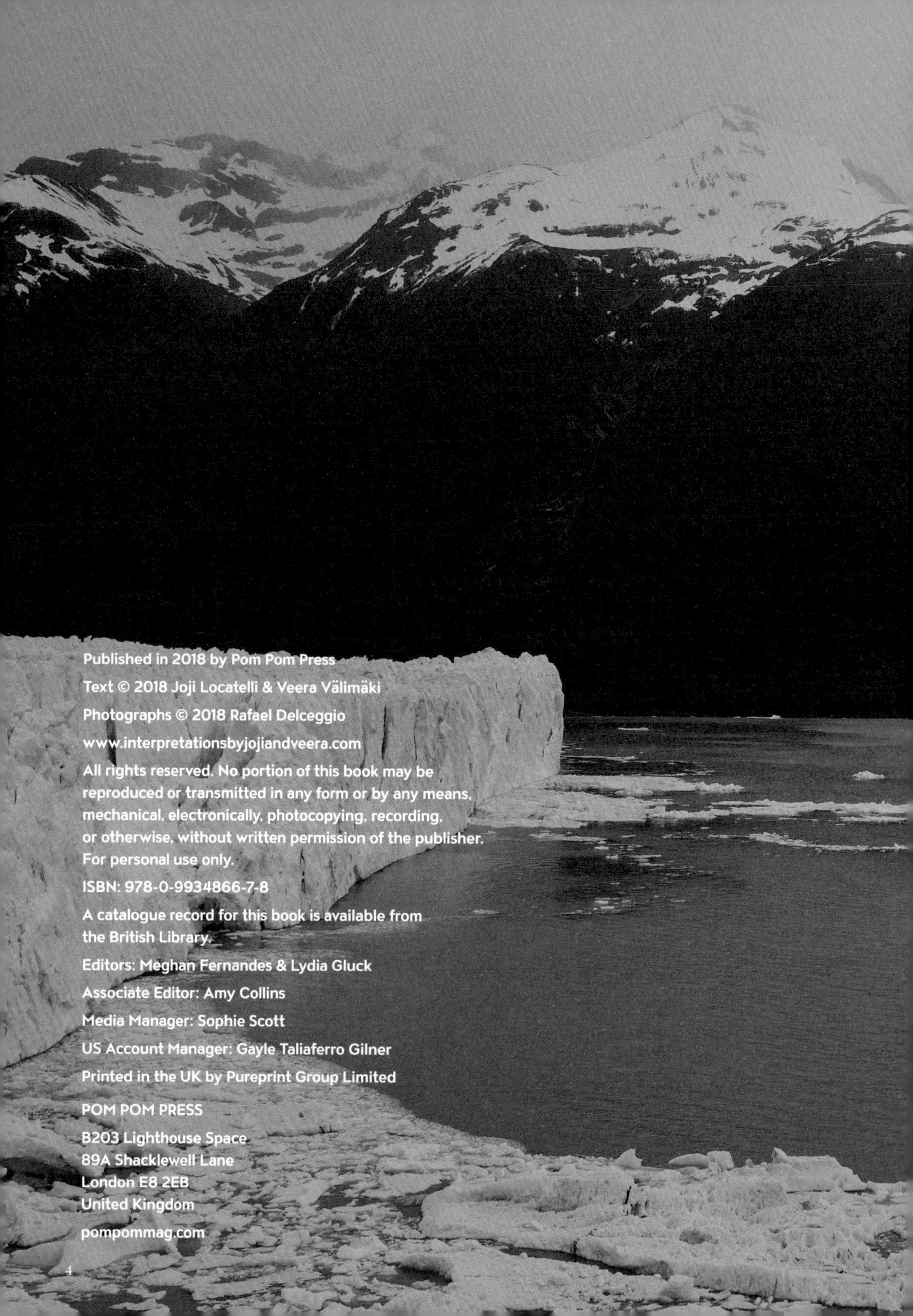

Published in 2018 by Pom Pom Press

www.interpretationsbyjojiandveera.com

ISBN: 978-0-9934866-7-8

A catalogue record for this book is available from the British Library.

Editors: Meghan Fernandes & Lydia Gluck

Associate Editor: Amy Collins

Media Manager: Sophie Scott

US Account Manager: Gayle Taliaferro Gilner

Printed in the UK by Pureprint Group Limited

POM POM PRESS

B203 Lighthouse Space
89A Shacklewell Lane
London E8 2EB
United Kingdom

pompommag.com

contents

foreword

Opening before you is our fifth *Interpretations*. Five years seems an impossibly long time, and yet it still feels like our first book coming out. Every year we come together to pour everything we have into these collections. If you have read our previous volumes, then you know how passionate we are about these encounters. *Interpretations* is a journey that we hope you appreciate as you move from one book to the next.

This volume was carefully planned to include twelve spectacular designs. There's not a single piece that was designed quickly or to fill a spot. We consider them all individual jewels and as always we hope they'll bring joy to your needles and wardrobe. There is something for each season, for each kind of knitter and for every woman's own style.

Everything has evolved in these five years: we have reached a certain confidence as designers that might not have been there before. We have matured in age and also in our minds, but without losing the adventurous spirit that we share and that always feels like a teenager pushing from within.

What is the same? The core, the passion, the feeling. Again, we chose six words to use as a starting point for our diverging interpretations and patterns: Bliss, Ground, Shelter, Movement, Explore and Rough.

Projects like these take support and without our advocates we couldn't convey our ideas so effortlessly. Rafael Delceggio, an old friend, captured our pieces with such magic in each photo... It's almost as if part of the light we experienced in Patagonia is trapped within each image. And as always, our good friend Jenica Poduje, a true poet, inspired us with her beautiful words. You will find her texts at the beginning of each theme.

What is new? We wanted this anniversary issue to be something even more extraordinary and decided to celebrate with special colors of yarn, created specifically for our collection. We collaborated with twelve immensely talented dyers and are forever grateful to all of them. Every yarn and colorway was a perfect interpretation of our mood and each of them turned out to be so much more than just the idea we had in the first place.

This year the dreamlike photoshoot happened in a place neither of us had ever seen. We traveled back to Argentina, but instead of staying in the centre of the country, near the capital, Buenos Aires, we traveled all the way South, to Patagonia and into wilderness.

The breathtaking surroundings, forests, mountains and glaciers, complimented the variety of our pieces as well as the different ways we reflect on each theme. On our photoshoot with Rafael, quietly exploring the mountaneous terrain, we felt bliss under the shelter of trees. We moved amongst the wild dancing waters, and felt grounded while burying our feet in an endless sea of smooth pebbles.

Therefore, we feel short of words to introduce you to this fifth anniversary *Interpretations*. We hope you will feel transported, as if you are traveling with us on our adventures, get your needles and yarn ready!

joji and veera

quiet stars cardigan

joy cardigan

indigo pullover

separate ways sweater

anemone top

dynamic trio shawl

free seeker wrap

rose quartz cardigan

glacier tunic

chasing light shawl

rugged coat

reflection shawl

bliss

leaning my head back against the tree, I close and rest my tired eyes. The sun drenches me completely in its freckling rays. I let my thoughts go as the sun melts into my skin leaving droplets of sun light on my face.

I feel sleep coming on and, in a weak effort to fight it, I breathe deeply inhaling the sweet anaesthesia, the fragrant air that surrounds me.

With a light heart, I dream of racing through the trees on a horse, limitless and free. The force of her steps lighten as her stride increases. We break through the curtains of trees into a clearing and race into the meadow before us. She senses home and throws her weight forward, faster than I think she's ever gone before. I feel her confidence and am unafraid.

I can smell the meadow, grass crushing beneath her step. The jolt of her hooves is gone and I open my eyes surprised to see the meadow far below us. In glorious amazement I take it all in and lift my arms high into the air.

As we ascend I notice, fantastically, I am holding a ribbon attached to an outrageous number of tiny white balloons. Feeling tranquil, my hand slackens and the little round balloons break away, scattering, in a race to the heavens. A cloud dissolving away.

A brief jolt and we have touched the ground. A jerk of my leg breaks the dream loose releasing its hold on me.

I'm blinded by the sun and covered in droplets of sweat, I blink and still see those white balloons adrift in my mind's eye. My troubles seem momentarily untangled and I'm feeling blissful, rested and full of hope.

bliss

joy cardigan

quiet stars cardigan

quiet stars

by joji locatelli

This delicate cardigan features a lace shawl collar and subtle patterning throughout the body. It is worked seamlessly from the top down using a clever construction.

I added ties to make it practical to wear, but you can leave them out and wear it open or use a pin to keep it closed.

quiet stars

Sizes

XS (S, M, L, XL, XXL, 3XL, 4XL). Shown in size M on a 36" bust.

To fit chest size 28/30 (34, 38, 42, 46, 50, 54, 58/60) inches [75/80 (85, 95, 105, 115, 125, 135, 145/150) cm]. Recommended ease: 0-2" [0-5 cm] of positive ease.

Bust circumference (with fronts overlapped and tied): 30 (34, 39, 42½ 46, 49, 55, 58)" [75 (85, 97.5, 106, 115, 122.5, 137.5, 145) cm]. *See schematics below and more finished measurements at the end of this pattern.*

Materials

Yarn: 4 (4, 4, 5, 5, 6, 6, 7) skeins of Fino by Julie Asselin (75% Merino, 15% Cashmere, 10% Silk; 400 yds [366 m] / 115 g) or approx. 1280 (1440, 1560, 1680, 1920, 2080, 2320, 2480) yds [1250 (1380, 1430, 1540, 1750, 1900, 2120, 2270) m] of fingering weight yarn. The sample was made using *Intepretations* special colorway Happy.

Needles: US 4 [3.5 mm] and US 2½ [3 mm] circular needles, 32" [80 cm] long.

Other: Stitch markers, stitch holders or waste yarn, tapestry needle.

Gauge

23.5 sts and 33 rows = 4" [10 cm] in Stockinette st on US 4 [3.5 mm] needles. *Before you measure, please take the time to wash and block your swatch in the same manner that you will wash and block your sweater.*

Finished Measurements

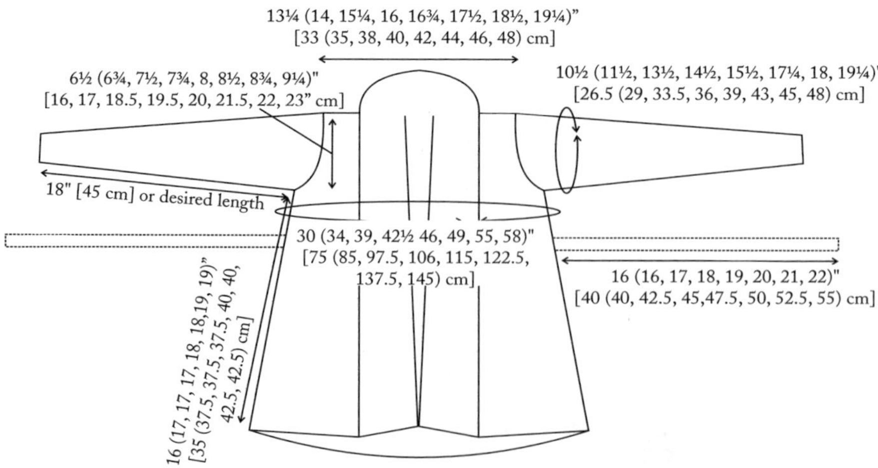

quiet stars

Stitches Used

Lace Repeat (LR) - worked flat over 9 sts

Row 1 (RS): Ssk, k1, yo, k3, yo, k1, k2tog.

Rows 2, 4, 6: P9

Row 3: K1, ssk, k1, yo, k1, yo, k1, k2tog, k1.

Row 5: K9

Repeat ***Rows 1-6*** for pattern.

Spots - worked flat over a multiple of 4 sts

Row 1: K3, p1.

Rows 2, 4, 6, 8: P4

Row 3: K4

Row 5: K1, p1, k2.

Row 7: K4

Repeat ***Rows 1-8*** for pattern.

Spots - worked in the round over a multiple of 4 sts

Round 1: K3, p1.

Rounds 2, 3, 4, 6, 7, 8: K4

Round 5: K1, p1, k2.

Repeat ***Rounds 1-8*** for pattern.

Directions

Right Collar

With US 4 [3.5 mm] needles, CO 26 (26, 30, 30, 30, 30, 35, 35) sts using a long tail cast on.

Row 1 (RS): K to end.

Row 2 (WS): P to end.

Row 3: (K1, m1L) to 1 st from end, then (according to your size) k1 (k1, k1fb, k1fb, k1fb, k1fb, k1, k1). *You should now have 51, (51, 60, 60, 60, 60, 69, 69) sts on the needles.*

Row 4: K3, p to end.

Row 5: K3, work row 1 of Lace Repeat (*LR - see Stitches Used*) 5 (5, 6, 6, 6, 6, 7, 7) times, k3.

Row 6: K3, work next row of LR 5 (5, 6, 6, 6, 6, 7, 7) times, p3.

Repeat ***Rows 5-6*** (always working the foll row of the LR until work measures 3½ (3½, 4, 4, 4, 4, 4½, 4½)" [9 (9, 10, 10, 10, 10, 11, 11) cm] from the CO edge, ending with a WS row. Break yarn and put all sts on hold. *Take note of what row of the repeat you end up on so you can work the other side to match.*

left Collar

With the RS facing you, pick up and knit 26 (26, 30, 30, 30, 30, 35, 35) sts from your CO edge.

Row 2 (WS): P to end.

Row 3: (K1, m1L) to 1 st from end, then (according to your size) k1 (k1, k1fb, k1fb, k1fb, k1fb, k1, k1). *You should now have 51, (51, 60, 60, 60, 60, 69, 69) sts on the needles.*

Row 4: P to 3 sts from end, k3.

Row 5: K3, work row 1 of LR 5 (5, 6, 6, 6, 6, 7, 7) times, k3.

Row 6: P3, work next row of LR 5 (5, 6, 6, 6, 6, 7, 7) times, k3.

Repeat ***Rows 5-6*** until work measures 3½ (3½, 4, 4, 4, 4, 4½, 4½)" [9 (9, 10, 10, 10, 10, 11, 11) cm] from the point where you picked up your stitches. Finish on the same row of the pattern repeat as you did for the other half of the collar. Break yarn and put all sts on hold.

Back

With US 4 [3.5 mm] needles and using the knitted cast on method, CO 16 (18, 20, 23, 24, 28, 27, 30) sts. With the RS facing you, pick up and knit 45 (45, 49, 47, 49, 49, 55, 53) sts from the Stockinette stitch edge of your collar (not from the Garter stitch edge). Using the knitted cast on method, CO 16 (18, 20, 23, 24, 28, 27, 30) more sts. *You should now have 77 (81, 89, 93, 97, 105, 109, 113) sts on the needles.*

Row 1 (WS): P to end.

Row 2 (RS): Work in Spots (*see Stitches used*) to 1 st from end, k1.

Repeat ***Rows 1-2*** until work measures 5½ (6, 6¼, 6¾, 6¾, 7½, 7¼,7 ½)" [14 (15, 15.5, 17, 17, 18.5, 18, 18.5) cm] from the CO edge, ending with a WS row.

Armhole Shaping

Row 1 (RS): CO 2, work in patt to end.

Row 2 (WS): CO 2, p to end.

Repeat ***Rows 1-2*** 1 (1, 3, 2, 3, 3, 5, 6) more times.

Next row (RS): CO 1 (2, 2, 4, 2, 2, 4, 5) sts. Knit all the stitches wrapping the yarn twice around the needle.

Next row (WS): CO 1 (2, 2, 4, 2, 2, 4, 5). Knit the sts you just cast on. Knit the 1st wrap of the next st leaving the 2nd wrap on the needle, *knit 2nd wrap together with 1st wrap of the next st*, repeat from * to last st, k1. *You should now have 87 (93, 109, 113, 117, 125, 141, 151) sts on the needles.*

Break yarn and put all sts on hold.

Right Front

Starting at the sleeve edge, pick up and knit 16 (18, 20, 23, 24, 28, 27, 30) sts along the right shoulder. Place the sts you had on hold for the Right Collar on the needles. K3, pm, work the foll row of LR to 3 sts from end, k3. *You should now have 67 (69, 80, 83, 84, 88, 96, 99) sts on the needle.*

Row 1 (WS): K3, p to m, sm, k1, p to end.

Row 2 (RS): K1, work in Spots to 1 st from m (*it is not necessary to finish the last repeat of the Spots patt*), p1, sm, work LR to 3 sts from end, k3.

Repeat ***Rows 1-2*** until work measures 5½ (6, 6¼, 6¾, 6¾, 7½, 7¼,7 ½)" [14 (15, 15.5, 17, 17, 18.5, 18, 18.5) cm] from the point where you picked up your sts, ending with a WS row.

Armhole Shaping

Row 1 (RS): CO2, work in patt to end, making sure that your spots pattern matches your previous work.

Row 2 (WS): Work in patt to end.

Repeat ***Rows 1-2*** 1 (1, 3, 3, 3, 3, 5, 6) more times. *You should now have 71 (73, 88, 91, 92, 96, 108, 113) sts on the needle.* Break yarn and put all sts on hold.

left Front

Place the sts you had on hold for the Left Collar on the needle. K3, work the foll row of LR to 3 sts from end, pm, k3. With the right needle, pick up and knit 16 (18, 20, 23, 24, 28, 27, 30) sts along the the left shoulder. *You should have 67 (69, 80, 83, 84, 88, 96, 99) sts on the needle.*

Row 1 (WS): P to 1 st from m, k1, sm, p to 3 sts from end, k3.

Row 2 (RS): K3, work LR to m, sm, p1, work in Spots to 1 st from end (*it is not necessary to finish the last repeat of the Spots patt*), k1.

Repeat ***Rows 1-2*** until work measures 5½ (6, 6¼, 6¾, 6¾, 7½, 7¼,7 ½)" [14 (15, 15.5, 17, 17, 18.5, 18, 18.5) cm] from the point where you picked up your sts, ending with the same WS row of the LR as you did for the other front.

Armhole Shaping

Row 1 (RS): Work in patt to end.

Row 2 (WS): CO2, work in patt to end.

Repeat ***Rows 1-2*** 1 (1, 3, 3, 3, 3, 5, 6) more times. *You should now have 71 (73, 88, 91, 92, 96, 108, 113) sts on the needle.*

Join Body

Row 1 (RS): K3, work in LR to m, sm, p1, work in Spots to 1 st from end, k1. CO 1 (1, 2, 5, 6, 6, 7, 7) sts, pm, CO 1 (3, 4, 6, 9, 10, 11, 10) sts. Place the sts you had on hold for the back on the needles and knit to end of row. CO 2 (3, 4, 7, 9, 9, 10, 10) sts, pm, CO 1 (1, 2, 5, 6, 6, 7, 7) sts. Place the sts you had on hold for the Right Front on the needle. K1, work in Spots Repeat to 1 sts from m, p1, sm, work in LR to 3 sts from end, k3.

You should now have a total of 234 (247, 297, 318, 331, 348, 392, 411) sts: 72 (74, 90, 96, 98, 102, 115, 120) sts for each front and 90 (99, 117, 126, 135, 144, 162, 171) sts for the back.

Row 2 (WS): K3, p to m, sm, k1, p to 1 st before last m (*slipping all other markers*), k1, sm, p to 3 sts from end, k3.

Row 3 (RS): K3, work in LR to m, sm, p1, work in Spots to m (*no need to finish the last repeat of the Spots patt*), sm, work LR (*starting on the same row as you are at the fronts*) 10 (11, 13, 14, 15, 16, 18, 19) times, sm, work in Spots to 1 st from m, p1, sm, work in LR to 3 sts from end, k3.

Repeat ***Rows 2-3*** 6 times and then work ***Row 2*** once more.

Next row (RS): K3, work in LR to m, sm, p1, work in Spots to m, sm, [work LR, pm] 9 (10, 12, 13, 14, 15, 17, 18) times, work LR, sm, work in Spots to 1 st from m, p1, sm, work Lace Repeat to 3 sts from end, k3.

Next row: Same as row 2.

Increase Row 1

Row 1 (RS): K3, work in LR to m, sm, p1, work in Spots to m, sm, m1L, [work LR, sm, m1L] 9 (10, 12, 13, 14, 15, 17, 18) times, work LR, m1L, sm, work in Spots to 1 st from m, p1, sm, work Lace Repeat to 3 sts from end, k3.

Row 2 (WS): K3, p to m, sm, k1, p to 1 st from last marker (*slipping all the other markers*), k1, sm, p to 3 sts from end, k3.

Row 3: K3, work in LR to m, sm, p1, work in Spots to m, sm, k1, [work LR, sm, k1] 9 (10, 12, 13, 14, 15, 17, 18) times, work LR, k1, sm, work in Spots to 1 st from m, p1, sm, work Lace Repeat to 3 sts from end, k3.

Row 4: K3, p to m, sm, k1, p to 1 st from last marker (*slipping all the other markers*), k1, sm, p to 3 sts from end, k3.

Repeat ***Rows 3-4*** 13 more times.

Increase Row 2

Row 1 (RS): K3, work in LR to m, sm, p1, work in Spots to m, sm, m1R, k1, m1L, [work LR, sm, m1R, k1, m1L] 9 (10, 12, 13, 14, 15, 17, 18) times, work LR, m1R, k1, m1L, sm, work in Spots to 1 st from m, p1, sm, work Lace Repeat to 3 sts from end, k3.

Row 2 (WS): K3, p to m, sm, k1, p to 1 st from last marker (slipping all the other markers), k1, sm, p to 3 sts from end, k3.

Row 3: K3, work in LR to m, sm, p1, work in Spots to m, sm, k3, [work LR, sm, k3] 9 (10, 12, 13, 14, 15, 17, 18) times, work LR, k3, sm, work in Spots to 1 st from m, p1, sm, work Lace Repeat to 3 sts from end, k3.

Row 4: K3, p to m, sm, k1, p to 1 st from last marker (*slipping all the other markers*), k1, sm, p to 3 sts from end, k3.

Repeat ***Rows 3-4*** 13 more times.

Increase row 3

Row 1 (RS): K3, work in LR to m, sm, p1, work in Spots to m, sm, m1R, k3, m1L, [work LR, sm, m1R, k3, m1L] 9 (10, 12, 13, 14, 15, 17, 18) times, work LR, m1R, k3, m1L, sm, work in Spots to 1 st from m, p1, sm, work Lace Repeat to 3 sts from end, k3.

Row 2 (WS): K3, p to m, sm, k1, p to 1 st from last marker (slipping all the other markers), k1, sm, p to 3 sts from end, k3.

Row 3: K3, work in LR to m, sm, p1, work in Spots to m, sm, k5, [work LR, sm, k5] 9 (10, 12, 13, 14, 15, 17, 18) times, work LR, k5, sm, work in Spots to 1 st from m, p1, sm, work Lace Repeat to 3 sts from end, k3.

Row 4: K3, p to m, sm, k1, p to 1 st from last marker (slipping all the other markers), k1, sm, p to 3 sts from end, k3.

Repeat ***Rows 3-4*** until work measures 14 (15, 15, 15, 16, 16, 17, 17)" [35 (37.5, 37.5, 37.5, 40, 40, 42.5, 42.5) cm] from the armhole, or 2" [5 cm] less than your desired length.

Bottom Shaping

Row 1 (RS): Work in patt (*as you were working previously*) to 12 sts from end, k5, W&T.

Row 2 (RS): Work in patt to 12 sts from end, p5, W&T.

Row 3: K5, work in patt to 12 sts from end, W&T.

Row 4: Work in patt to 12 sts from end, W&T.

Row 5: Work in patt to 9 sts before last wrapped st, W&T.

Row 6: Work in patt to 9 sts before last wrapped st, W&T.

Repeat ***Rows 5-6*** 2 (2, 3, 3, 3, 3, 4, 4) more times.

Next row (RS): Work in patt to last m, sm, k to end of row picking up the wraps as you find them.

Next row (WS): Work in patt to last m, sm, p to 3 sts from end of row picking up the wraps as you find them, k3.

Switch to US 2 ½ [3mm] needles.

Next row (RS):

Sizes XS (L, XXL and 3XL): Sl1, p2tog, k1, (p1, k1) to end.

Sizes S (M, XL, 4XL): K1, (p1, k1) to end.

Next row (WS): K1, (k1, p1) to 2 sts from end, k2.

Work 4 more rows in the established ribbing.

BO all sts in pattern using the larger needles.

Sleeves

With larger needles, starting at the centre of the bottom of the armhole, pick up and knit 61 (69, 79, 85, 91, 101, 105, 113) sts around the armhole. Pm and join for working in the round.

Row 1: K38 (44, 49, 54, 59, 66, 70, 76), W&T.

Row 2: P15 (19, 19, 23, 27, 31, 35, 37), W&T.

Row 3: (K3, p1) to 3 sts before last wrapped st, k3, knit next st with wrap, W&T.

Row 4: P to last wrapped st and purl it with wrap, W&T.

Row 5: K to last wrapped st and knit it with wrap, W&T.

Row 6: P to last wrapped st and purl it with wrap, W&T.

Row 7: Work in Spots (*adjusting your stitches so it matches your work in Round 3*) to last wrapped st, knit it together with its corresponding wrap, W&T.

Row 8: P to last wrapped st and purl it with wrap, W&T.

Repeat ***Rows 7-8*** until approx. 5 sts remain at each side of the marker.

Next round: Work in Spots to end of round, picking up last wrap as you find it.

Work 16 rounds in Spots pattern.

Next round - Decrease round: K1, ssk, work in patt to 3 sts from end, k2tog, k1.

Continue working in pattern repeating a decrease round every 12th (8th, 8th, 7th, 6th, 6th, 5th, 4th) following round 7 (11, 11, 14, 17, 18, 20, 24) more times. *You should have 45 (45, 55, 55, 55, 63, 63, 63) sts.*

When sleeve measures 14" [35 cm] switch to US 2½ [3 mm] needles.

Sizes M, L and XL only:

Next round: K2tog, k to end of round. *54 sts left.*

All sizes:

Start cuff repeat:

Round 1 (RS): (Ssk, k1, yo, k3, yo, k1, k2tog) to end.

Round 2: K to end

Round 3: (K1, ssk, k1, yo, k1, yo, k1, k2tog, k1) to end.

Round 4: K to end.

Repeat ***Rounds 1-4*** 8 more times, or until cuff measures 4" [10 cm] or until you reach your desired length.

BO all sts loosely.

Finishing

Weave in all ends and block sweater to measurements.

Once the sweater is blocked and dry, try the sweater on and mark the placement on each side where you want your ties to start. I started mine about 4" [10 cm] down from the armhole.

With smaller needles -US 2 ½ [3mm]- pick up 11 sts from the side of the sweater. Make sure that all these sts are vertically aligned. Join yarn and start ties:

Row 1: Sl1, (p1, k1) to end.

Row 2: Sl1, (k1, p1) to end.

Repeat these 2 rows until your tie measures approx. 16 (16, 17, 18, 19, 20, 21, 22)" [40 (40, 42.5, 45,47.5, 50, 52.5, 55) cm]. Bind off all sts and repeat for the other tie.

Finished Measurements

Bust circumference (with fronts overlapped and tied): 30 (34, 39, 42½ 46, 49, 55, 58)" [75 (85, 97.5, 106, 115, 122.5, 137.5, 145) cm].

Cross back: 13¼ (14, 15¼, 16, 16¾, 17½, 18½, 19¼)" [33 (35, 38, 40, 42, 44, 46, 48) cm].

Armhole depth: 6½ (6¾, 7½, 7¾, 8, 8½, 8¾, 9¼)" [16 (17, 18.5, 19.5, 20, 21.5, 22, 23) cm].

Upper sleeve circumference: 10½ (11½, 13½, 14½, 15½, 17¼, 18, 19¼)" [26.5 (29, 33.5, 36, 39, 43, 45, 48) cm].

Sleeve length underarm to cuff: 18" [45 cm] or desired length.

Length from underarm to bottom hem: 16 (17, 17, 17, 18, 18, 19, 19)" [35 (37.5, 37.5, 37.5, 40, 40, 42.5, 42.5) cm].

joy

by veera välimäki

This little cardigan will keep your needles happily clicking while you enjoy every turn and yarnover of the lace! Simple clear yoke design and subtle waist shaping make this cardigan very easy to wear and very feminine. The delicate minty color soothes your eyes and makes this cardigan total bliss to knit. There is no better name for this design than Joy.

joy

Sizes

XS (S, M, L, XL, 2XL). Shown in size M on a 36½" bust.

Finished chest circumference (buttoned): 32 (36, 40, 44, 48, 52)" [80 (90, 100, 110, 120, 130) cm]. Choose size with a small amount of positive ease.

Materials

Yarn: 3 (3, 3, 4, 4, 4) skeins of Titus 4ply by Eden Cottage Yarns (75% Superwash Merino Wool, 25% Silk; 436 yds [400 m] / 100 g). Approx. 1020 (1140, 1280, 1400, 1530, 1670) yds [930 (1040, 1170, 1280, 1400, 1530) m] of fingering weight yarn. The sample was knit in *Interpretations* special colorway called Bliss.

Needles: US 6 [4 mm] and US 4 [3.5 mm] circular needle, 32" [80 cm] long, and dpns in each size. Adjust needle size if necessary to obtain the correct gauge.

Other: 8 (8, 9, 9, 10, 10) ½" [1 cm] buttons. Stitch markers, stitch holders or waste yarn, tapestry needle and blocking aids. Optional, but highly recommended: row counter.

Gauge

24 sts and 30 rows = 4" [10 cm] in Stockinette stitch using larger needles.

Finished Measurements

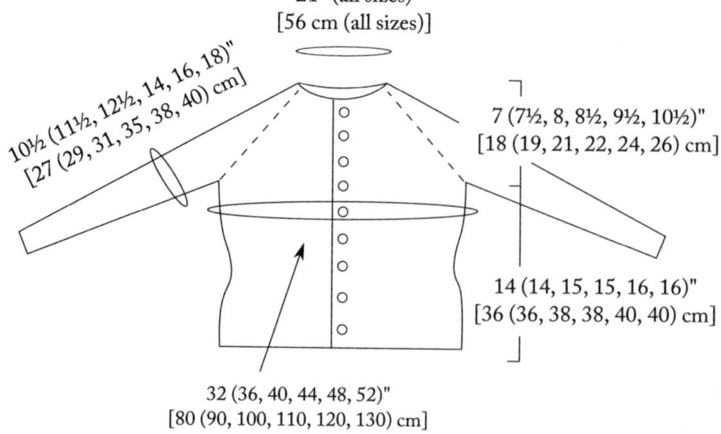

joy

Collar

Using smaller circular needle and long-tail cast on, CO 142 sts. Do not join. *Note: All sizes start with the same number.*

Purl the first row (WS). Work 4 rows back and forth in twisted ribbing ([k1 tbl, p1 tbl] to end of row).

Work first buttonhole on next row (RS): Work in twisted ribbing to last 6 sts, knit the next 2 sts together tbl (twisting the stitches for continuous twisted ribbing), yo, [k1 tbl, p1 tbl] to end.

Work 3 more rows in twisted ribbing.

Yoke

Change to larger circular needle, begin short row shaping and place markers on next row as follows.

Row 1 (RS, short row): [K1 tbl, p1 tbl] the first 10 sts (continuous twisted ribbing), knit 13 sts, m1R, pm, k30, pm, m1L, k36, m1R, pm, k30, pm, m1L, k1, W&T.

Row 2 (WS, short row): Purl to m, m1L (purl), sm, p to m, sm, m1R (purl), purl to m, m1L (purl), sm, purl to m, sm, m1R (purl), p1, W&T.

Row 3 (RS, short row): Knit to m, m1R, sm, k to m, sm, m1L, knit to m, m1R, sm, knit to m, sm, m1L, knit to previous wrapped st, k2tog the wrap and the wrapped st (making sure the wrap stays on WS), W&T.

Row 4 (WS, short row): Purl to m, m1L (purl), sm, p to m, sm, m1R (purl), purl to m, m1L (purl), sm, purl to m, sm, m1R (purl), purl to previous wrapped st, ssp the wrap with the wrapped st (making sure the wrap stays on WS), W&T.

Repeat ***Rows 3 and 4*** – 4 (5, 6, 6, 6, 6) more times. *You should have 190 (198, 206, 206, 206, 206) sts on needle.*

Work to end on Next Row (RS): Knit to m, m1R, sm, k to m, sm, m1L, knit to m, m1R, sm, knit to m, sm, m1L, knit to previous wrapped st, k2tog the wrap and the wrapped st (making sure the wrap stays on WS), knit to last 10 sts, [k1 tbl, p1 tbl] the last 10 sts.

Next Row (WS) –

Only size XS (no increases): [K1 tbl, p1 tbl] the first 10 sts (continuous twisted ribbing), purl to m, sm, p to m, sm, purl to m, sm, purl to m, sm, purl to previous wrapped st, ssp the wrap with the wrapped st (making sure the wrap stays on WS), purl to last 10 sts, [k1 tbl, p1 tbl] the last 10 sts.

All other sizes: [K1 tbl, p1 tbl] the first 10 sts (continuous twisted ribbing), purl to m, m1L (purl), sm, p to m, sm, m1R (purl), purl to m, m1L (purl), sm, purl to m, sm, m1R (purl), purl to previous wrapped st, ssp the wrap with the wrapped st (making sure the wrap stays on WS), purl to last 10 sts, [k1 tbl, p1 tbl] the last 10 sts.

You should have 194 (206, 214, 214, 214, 214) sts on needle.

Sizes XS and S only

Continue with raglan increases and add lace panels next:

Next Row (RS): [K1 tbl, p1 tbl] the first 10 sts (continuous twisted ribbing), k6, pm for lace, work row 1 of Chart A, pm for lace, knit to 1 st before marker, m1R, k1, sm, k1, m1L, knit to 1 st before marker, m1R, k1, sm, k1, m1L, knit 7 (9), pm for lace, work row 1 of Chart A 3 times, pm for lace, knit to 1 st before marker, m1R, k1, sm, k1, m1L, knit to 1 st before marker, m1R, k1, sm, k1, m1L, knit to last 31 sts, pm for lace, work row 1 of Chart A, pm for lace, k5, [k1 tbl, p1 tbl] the last 10 sts.

Next Row (WS): [K1 tbl, p1 tbl] the first 10 sts (continuous twisted ribbing), purl to m, sm (lace), work the next row of Chart A, sm (lace), purl to m, sm, p to m, sm, purl to m, sm (lace), work the next row of Chart A 3 times, sm (lace), purl to m, sm, purl to m, sm, purl to m, sm (lace), work the next row of Chart A, sm (lace), purl to last 10 sts, [k1 tbl, p1 tbl] the last 10 sts.

Chart A

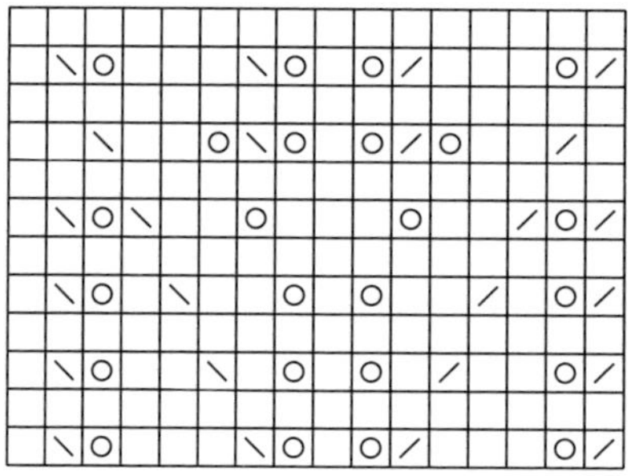

- St st; knit on RS, purl on WS
- Yarnover
- Ssk
- K2tog

Jump next to ***All Sizes*** paragraph.

Sizes M, L, XL and 2XL only

Continue with body increases as before and add lace panels:

Row A (RS): [K1 tbl, p1 tbl] the first 10 sts (continuous twisted ribbing), k6, pm for lace, work row 1 of Chart A, pm for lace, k to m, m1R, sm, k to m, sm, m1L, knit 12 (all sizes M, L, XL and 2XL), pm for lace, work row 1 of Chart A 3 times, pm for lace, knit 12 to marker, m1R, sm, k to m, sm, m1L, knit to last 31 sts, pm for lace, work row 1 of Chart A, pm for lace, k5, [k1 tbl, p1 tbl] the last 10 sts.

Row B (WS): [K1 tbl, p1 tbl] the first 10 sts (continuous twisted ribbing), purl to m, sm (lace), work the next row of Chart A, sm (lace), purl to m, m1L (purl), sm, p to m, sm, m1R (purl), purl to m, sm (lace), work the next row of Chart A 3 times, sm (lace), purl to m, m1L (purl), sm, p to m, sm, m1R (purl), purl to m, sm (lace), work the next row of Chart A, sm (lace), purl to last 10 sts, [k1 tbl, p1 tbl] the last 10 sts.

Row C (RS): [K1 tbl, p1 tbl] the first 10 sts (continuous twisted ribbing), knit to m, sm (lace), work the next row of Chart A, sm (lace), k to m, m1R, sm, k to m, sm, m1L, k to m, sm (lace), work the next row of Chart A 3 times, sm (lace), k to m, m1R, sm, k to m, sm, m1L, k tom, sm (lace), work the next row of Chart A, sm (lace), k5, [k1 tbl, p1 tbl] the last 10 sts.

Only Size M: jump to paragraph called ***Sizes M and L only.***

Row D (WS): [K1 tbl, p1 tbl] the first 10 sts (continuous twisted ribbing), purl to m, sm (lace), work the next row of Chart A, sm (lace), purl to m, m1L (purl), sm, p to m, sm, m1R (purl), purl to m, sm (lace), work the next row of Chart A 3 times, sm (lace), purl to m, m1L (purl), sm, p to m, sm, m1R (purl), purl to m, sm (lace), work the next row of Chart A, sm (lace), purl to last 10 sts, [k1 tbl, p1 tbl] the last 10 sts.

Size L: Repeat the Row C once, and then jump to next paragraph called ***Sizes M and L only.***

Sizes XL and 2XL: Repeat Rows C and D once (XL) or twice (2XL). Jump next to ***All Sizes*** paragraph.

Sizes M and L only

Next Row (WS): [K1 tbl, p1 tbl] the first 10 sts (continuous twisted ribbing), purl to m, sm (lace), work the next row of Chart A, sm (lace), purl to m, sm, p to m, sm, purl to m, sm (lace), work the next row of Chart A 3 times, sm (lace), purl to m, sm, purl to m, sm, purl to m, sm (lace), work the next row of Chart A, sm (lace), purl to last 10 sts, [k1 tbl, p1 tbl] the last 10 sts.

Jump next to ***All Sizes*** paragraph.

All sizes

Row 5 (RS): [K1 tbl, p1 tbl] the first 10 sts (continuous twisted ribbing), knit to m, sm (lace), work the next row of Chart A, sm (lace), knit to 1 st before marker, m1R, k1, sm, k1, m1L, knit to 1 st before marker, m1R, k1, sm, k1, m1L, knit to m, sm (lace), work the next row of Chart A 3 times, sm (lace), knit to 1 st before marker, m1R, k1, sm, k1, m1L, knit to 1 st before marker, m1R, k1, sm, k1, m1L, knit to m, sm (lace), work the next row of Chart A, sm (lace), knit to last 10 sts, [k1 tbl, p1 tbl] the last 10 sts and at the same time, every 2¼" [6 cm] make a buttonhole as in collar.

Row 6 (WS): [K1 tbl, p1 tbl] the first 10 sts (continuous twisted ribbing), purl to m, sm (lace), work the next row of Chart A, sm (lace), purl to m, sm, p to m, sm, purl to m, sm (lace), work the next row of Chart A 3 times, sm (lace), purl to m, sm, purl to m, sm, purl to m, sm (lace), work the next row of Chart A, sm (lace), purl to last 10 sts, [k1 tbl, p1 tbl] the last 10 sts.

Repeat ***Rows 5 and 6*** – 10 (12, 14, 17, 20, 22) more times. *You should have 290 (318, 346, 378, 406, 430) sts on needle.*

Divide for body and sleeves

Next row (RS): [K1 tbl, p1 tbl] the first 10 sts (continuous twisted ribbing), knit to m, sm, work the next row of Chart A, sm, knit to m, remove m, place the stitches before next marker on holder for sleeve, CO 5 (6, 6, 7, 9, 11), pm for side, CO 5 (6, 6, 7, 9, 11), remove m, knit to m, sm (lace), work the next row of Chart A 3 times, sm (lace), knit to m, remove m, place the stitches before next marker on holder for sleeve, CO 5 (6, 6, 7, 9, 11), pm for side, CO 5 (6, 6, 7, 9, 11), remove m, knit to m, sm (lace), work the next row of Chart A, sm (lace), knit to last 10 sts, [k1 tbl, p1 tbl] the last 10 sts and at the same time, make buttonhole if necessary in your size (every 2¼" [6 cm]).

You should have 202 (226, 250, 274, 298, 322) sts on needle for body and 54 (58, 60, 66, 72, 76) sts on each holder for sleeves.

Body

Continue with body stitches on needle. Work even in St st and lace patterns as established, with button bands in twisted ribbing ([k1 tbl, p1 tbl] the first and last 10 sts), until the body measures 3 (3½, 4, 4, 4½, 4½)" [8 (9, 10, 10, 12, 12) cm] from underarm. Continue working buttonholes every 2¼" [6 cm] as in collar.

Begin waist shaping.

Decrease row (RS): [K1 tbl, p1 tbl] the first 10 sts (continuous twisted ribbing), knit to m, sm (lace), work the next row of Chart A, sm (lace), knit to 7 sts before m, k2tog, k5, sm, k5, ssk, knit to m, sm (lace), work the next row of Chart A 3 times, sm (lace), knit to 7 sts before m, k2tog, k5, sm, k5, ssk, knit to m, sm (lace), work the next row of Chart A, sm (lace), knit to last 10 sts, [k1 tbl, p1 tbl] the last 10 sts and at the same time, make buttonhole if necessary in your size (every 2¼" [6 cm]).

Repeat the ***Decrease Row*** 3 more times every 4th row (every 2nd RS row). Work 2" [5 cm] even as established.

Increase row (RS): [K1 tbl, p1 tbl] the first 10 sts (continuous twisted ribbing), knit to m, sm (lace), work the next row of Chart A, sm (lace), knit to 6 sts before m, m1R, k6, sm, k6, m1L, knit to m, sm (lace), work the next row of Chart A 3 times, sm (lace), knit to 6 sts before m, m1R, k6, sm, k6, m1L, knit to m, sm (lace), work the next row of Chart A, sm (lace), knit to last 10 sts, [k1 tbl, p1 tbl] the last 10 sts and at the same time, make buttonhole if necessary in your size (every 2¼" [6 cm]).

Repeat the ***Increase Row*** 3 more times every 4th row (every 2nd RS row). Continue even until the body measures 12½" [32 cm] from underarm.

Continue in St st and button bands in twisted ribbing only (no more lace) until the body measures 14 (14, 14½, 14½, 15, 15)" [36 (36, 37, 37, 38, 38) cm] from underarm.

Change to smaller circular needle. Work 1½" [4 cm] in twisted ribbing and work the last buttonhole as established at latest in centre of the hem ribbing. BO body stitches in pattern.

Sleeves

Place 54 (58, 60, 66, 72, 76) sleeve sts on larger dpns. Attach yarn to centre of the underarm CO stitches and pick up and knit 5 (6, 8, 9, 11, 13) sts to stitches on needles, knit sleeve sts, pick up and knit 5 (6, 8, 9, 11, 13) sts to centre of underarm. Place a BOR marker. *You should have 64 (70, 76, 84, 94, 102) stitches on needle. Note: You will pick up more stitches than you cast-on for the body in some sizes; do not decrease any of these stitches.*

Work in St st until the sleeve measures 2" [5 cm] from underarm. Begin decreases:

> ***Decrease Round (RS):*** K2, ssk, knit to last 4 sts, k2tog, k2.

Repeat ***Decrease Round*** every 1¼" [3 cm] for 6 (7, 8, 9, 10, 11) more times. *You should have 50 (54, 58, 64, 72, 78) stitches on needle.* Continue even until the sleeve measures 16" [40 cm] from underarm.

Change to smaller dpns and work 2" [5 cm] in twisted ribbing. BO sleeve stitches in pattern.

Finishing

Sew on all buttons carefully. Weave in all yarn ends and block the cardigan using your preferred method.

ground

In my favorite chair I sit, in my own little corner of time. Unnoticed, for now, all indecision slips away and my creativity flows like a rushing river.

I'm a suspect in my own mystery as I wonder what shall come next and how it will end.

Time runs quickly in this place and soon other duties will draw me away. For now, this is where it all happens and everything begins to unfold.

My emotions are smoke and mirrors, the truth starving me from a sense of relaxation. My nerves are like sparks, ready to flare up at any moment; ready to run if need be, this moment could be quick and fleeting.

For now, this creativity taking hold of me, has me rooted in this spot. This is where I'm grounded, connected to my soul and I feel most alive.

I'll show you how the mystery ends, the idea shoots, like a root taking hold, curling around my needles. Then, you too can begin to gain ground on a whole new creation of your own. Our ideas unfolding together like petals, as a new bloom emerges.

Now, my tribe calls and I must leave this spot, until I can find a way to return another day.

ground

indigo pullover

separate ways sweater

separate ways

by joji locatelli

Stripes inspire me in so many ways... There's something magical about them that makes projects fly off my needles. There's always just one more stripe to complete. In this design I explore stripes taking different directions and shapes.

This boxy-style sweater is flattering for every body shape with its loose flowing lines, its v-neck and its sweet subtle striping.

separate ways

Sizes

XS (S, M, L, XL, XXL, 3XL, 4XL). Shown in size M on a 36" bust.

To fit chest size 28/30 (34, 38, 42, 46, 50, 54, 58/60) inches [75/80 (85, 95, 105, 115, 125, 135, 145/150) cm]. The positive ease is built into the pattern. Choose a size according to your bust measurement and the list of sizes above. *See schematics below and more finished measurements at the end of this pattern.*

Materials

Yarn: 4 (4, 4, 5, 5, 8, 8, 8) skeins of Studio Sock by Neighborhood Fiber Co (100% Merino; 400 yds [366 m] / 114 g) or other fingering weight yarn in 4 different colors. The sample was made using 4 *Intepretations* special colorways.

Color 1: 1 (1, 1, 2, 2, 2, 2, 2) skeins or 280 (340, 400, 460, 520, 580, 640, 760) yds [256 (311, 366, 420, 475, 530, 585, 695) m]; shown in Navy.

Color 2: 1 (1, 1, 1, 1, 2, 2, 2) skeins or 240 (280, 320, 360, 400, 480, 520, 560) yds [220 (256, 292, 329, 366, 439, 475, 512) m]; shown in Brown Pink.

Color 3: 1 (1, 1, 1, 1, 2, 2, 2) skeins or 240 (280, 320, 360, 400, 480, 520, 560) yds [220 (256, 292, 329, 366, 439, 475, 512) m]; shown in Denim.

Color 4: 1 (1, 1, 1, 1, 2, 2, 2) skeins or 240 (280, 320, 360, 400, 480, 520, 560) yds [220 (256, 292, 329, 366, 439, 475, 512) m]; shown in Dark Gray.

Needles:US 4 [3.5 mm] and US 3 [3.25 mm] circular needles, 32" [80 cm] long.

Other: Stitch markers, stitch holders or waste yarn, tapestry needle.

Gauge

22 sts and 32 rows = 4" [10 cm] in Stockinette st on US 4 [3.5 mm] needles. *Before you measure, please take the time to wash and block your swatch in the same manner that you will wash and block your sweater.*

Finished Measurements

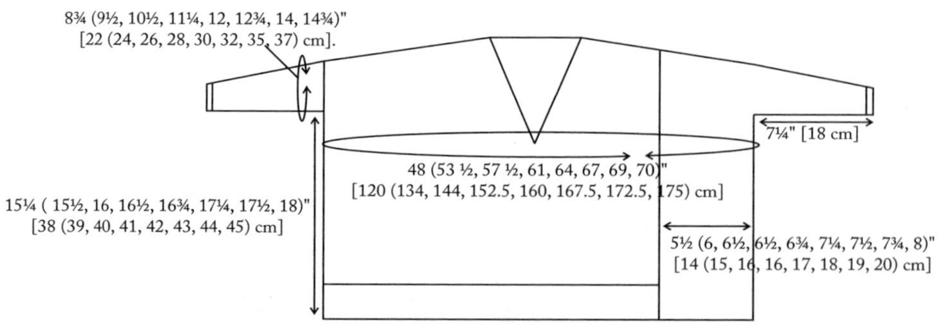

separate ways

Stitches Used

Body Stripe Sequence (Stockinette Stitch)

2 rows color 1. Do not break yarn color 1, always carry it up the side.

6 rows color 2. Break yarn.

2 rows color 1.

6 rows color 3. Break yarn.

2 rows color 1.

6 rows color 4. Break yarn.

Directions

left Front

With COLOR 4 and larger needles, CO 20 (26, 29, 32, 33, 33, 33, 31) sts.

Row 1 (RS): K to end.

Row 2 (WS) and all foll WS rows: P to end.

Row 3: K3, W&T.

Row 5: K2, m1R, k to last wrapped st and knit it with wrap, k4 (6, 7, 8, 8, 8, 8, 8), W&T.

Row 7: K to last wrapped st and knit it with wrap, k4 (6, 7, 8, 8, 8, 8, 8), W&T.

Row 9: Same as Row 5.

Row 11: K to last wrapped st and knit it with wrap. Knit to end of row.

Row 13: K2, m1R, k to end.

Work 7 more rows in Stockinette St, increasing at neck edge every 4th following row (as directed in row 13).

Break yarn and start working in the stripe sequence found at the beginning of the pattern. Continue increasing at neck edge. Increase on row 1 of the repeat and then on every 4th following row.

Work in this manner until you have increased a total of 15 (15, 16, 17, 18, 19, 20, 21) times since you started the Left Front - *you should have 35 (41, 45, 49, 51, 52, 53, 52) sts on the needles.* Work a WS row after your last increase row.

Break yarn and put all sts on hold.

Right Front

With COLOR 4 and larger needles, CO 51 (59, 64, 67, 70, 73, 75, 75) sts.

Row 1 (RS): K to end.

Row 2 (WS): P3, W&T.

Row 3: K to end.

Row 4: P to last wrapped st and purl it with wrap, p4 (6, 7, 8, 8, 8, 8, 8), W&T.

Row 5: K to 2 sts before end, m1L, k2.

Row 6: P to last wrapped st and purl it with wrap, p4 (6, 7, 8, 8, 8, 8, 8), W&T.

Row 7: K to end.

Row 8: P to last wrapped st and purl it with wrap, p4 (6, 7, 8, 8, 8, 8, 8), W&T.

Repeat ***Rows 5-8*** twice more.

Row 17: K to 2 sts before end, m1L, k2.

Row 18: P to last wrapped st and purl it together with wrap, k to end.

Work 2 more rows in Stockinette st. Break yarn and start working in the stripe sequence found at the beginning of the pattern. Continue increasing at neck edge. Increase on row 1 of the repeat and then then on every 4th following row.

Work in this manner until work measures 4½ (4¾, 5¼, 5½, 6, 6½, 7, 7½)" [11 (12, 13, 14, 15, 16, 17.5, 18.5) cm] from the CO edge, measured along the shortest edge (the right sleeve edge), ending with a WS row. Keep in mind that for now, the right front will be shorter than the left.

Break yarn and put all sts on hold. Make note of what row of your stripe sequence you end on, so that you can work the back to the same length.

Back

With COLOR 4, pick up and knit 51 (59, 64, 67, 70, 73, 75, 75) sts along the CO edge of the Right Shoulder.

Row 2 (WS): P to end.

Row 3: K1, m1L, k2, W&T.

Row 4: P to end of row. Break yarn and put

these sts on hold.

With color 4, pick up and knit 20 (26, 29, 32, 33, 33, 33, 31) sts along the CO edge of the Left Shoulder.

Row 2 (WS): P3, W&T.

Row 3: K to 1 st from end, m1R, k1.

Row 4: P to last wrapped st, purl it with wrap, p4 (6, 7, 8, 8, 8, 8, 8), W&T.

Join Shoulders

Row 1 (RS): K to end, CO 28 (28, 30, 32, 34, 36, 38, 40) sts using backwards loop, place the sts you had on hold on the needle, knit to wrapped st, knit it with wrap, k4 (6, 7, 8, 8, 8, 8, 8), W&T. *You should have 101 (115, 125, 133, 139, 144, 148, 148) sts on the needle.*

Row 2 (WS): P to last wrapped st, purl it with its wrap, p4 (6, 7, 8, 8, 8, 8, 8), W&T.

Row 3: K to last wrapped st, knit it with its wrap, k4 (6, 7, 8, 8, 8, 8, 8), W&T.

Repeat ***Rows 2-3*** once.

Row 6: P to last wrapped st, purl it with wrap, p to end of row.

Row 7: Same as row 3.

Row 8: P to end.

Repeat ***Rows 7-8*** 3 more times.

Next row (RS): K to wrapped st, knit it with its wrap, k to end of row.

Next row (WS): P to end.

Break yarn and start working in the stripe sequence always in Stockinette St.

Work until your piece measures 4½ (4¾, 5¼, 5½, 6, 6½, 7, 7½)" [11 (12, 13, 14, 15, 16, 17.5, 18.5) cm] from the CO edge, measured along the shortest edge (the right sleeve edge), ending with a WS row. You should be on the same row of the stripe sequence as you ended up on for the Right Front.

Join Right Side

Next row (RS): K to end of row (following the stripe sequence). Place the sts you had on hold for the Right Front on the needles, and work in pattern to end of row.

Remember to work a neck increase if you need to make one on this row.

Next row: P to end of row.

Work in pattern keeping the stripe sequence until you have completed 15 (15, 16, 17, 18, 19, 20, 21) neck increases. *You should have 167 (189, 205, 217, 227, 236, 243, 244) sts on the needles.*

Work a WS row after your last neck increase row. You should be on the same row of the repeat as you finished on for the left front.

Join Fronts

Next row (RS): K to end of row. Place the sts you had on hold for the Left Front and place them on the needles. K to end of row. *You should now have 202 (230, 250, 266, 278, 288, 296, 296) sts on the needles.*

Next row: P to end of row.

Continue working straight, in pattern, keeping the stripe sequence until work measures 13 (13¼, 13¾, 14¼, 14½, 15, 15¼, 15¾)" [32 (33, 34, 35, 36, 37, 38, 39) cm] from armhole, ending with a band of COLOR 1.

Bottom Hem

Change to US 3 [3.25 mm] needles.

Next row (RS): (K1, p1) to end of row.

Next row (WS): (K1, p1) to end of row.

Work in the established ribbing for 2¼" [6 cm]. BO all sts loosely in pattern.

Vertical Piece

Vertical Stripe Sequence (Stockinette Stitch)

For a neater edge, I recommend breaking the yarn with every color change, but you can carry color 1 up if you prefer.

8 rows COLOR 2

2 rows COLOR 1

8 rows COLOR 4

2 rows COLOR 1

8 rows COLOR 3

2 rows COLOR 1

With US 4 [3.5mm] needles, starting at the corner of the hem at the front and with COLOR 2, pick up and knit 114 (118, 123, 128, 132, 137, 142, 146) sts along the front edge, pm, pick up and knit 114 (118, 123, 128, 132, 137, 142, 146) sts along the back edge, finishing at the corner of the back hem.

You should have 228 (236, 246, 256, 264, 274, 284, 292) sts. The approx. pick up ratio is 2 sts out of every 3 rows.

Next row (WS): K10, p to 10 sts from end of row, k10.

Next row (RS) - Shoulder decrease row: K to 3 sts from m, k2tog, k1, sm, k1, ssk, k to end.

Next row (WS): K10, p to 10 sts from end of row, k10.

Continue working in the Vertical Stripe Sequence (*found at the beginning of this section*) but repeat a shoulder decrease round every 8th (8th, 10th, 10th, 10th, 10th, 12th, 12th) row 4 more times.

Work in this manner until your work measures 5½ (6, 6½, 6½, 6¾, 7¼, 7½, 8)" [14 (15, 16, 16, 17, 18, 19, 20) cm], ending with a WS row. Note: You can end with any color except with color 1. If this is the case, work 2 more rows so that you end with a different color.

If you were knitting on straight needles, move your stitches to a circular needle in the same size as you were using. Break your working yarn leaving a 60" [150 cm] tail.

Now place both ends of the needle together (the wrong sides of the fabric facing each other) and with your working yarn and a tapestry needle graft 85 (86, 89, 92, 94, 97, 98, 100) sts from one end together with 85 (86, 89, 92, 94, 97, 98, 100) sts from the other end. This will form the side seam of your sweater. The remaining (un-grafted) stitches will represent your sleeve opening. Once you finish grafting these stitches, secure yarn and cut the remaining tail.

Left Sleeve

You should have 48 (54, 58, 62, 66, 70, 78, 82) stitches left on your needle with the shoulder marker in the middle of them. Join in the color that you last worked with and knit to the end of row, removing the shoulder marker and placing a new marker in the underarm. Join for working in the round.

Work in stockinette stitch for 8 rounds. You will no longer be using the Stripe sequence.

Next round - decrease round: K1, ssk, k to 3 sts from end, k2tog, k1.

Continue working in Stockinette stitch and repeat a decrease round every 8th following row.

When the sleeve measures 3" [7.5 cm] from where you joined in the round, switch to COLOR 1. Work 2 rounds. Switch to the next color in your sequence (in my sample COLOR 2).

Continue working in this color, repeating the decrease round every 8th following round until work measures 6" [15 cm] from the armhole.

Switch to US 3 [3.25 mm] needles.

Next round: (K1, p1) to end of round.

Work in the established ribbing for 12 rounds.

On the next round BO all sts in pattern.

Right Sleeve

Pick up and knit 48 (54, 58, 62, 66, 70, 78, 82) sts around the left sleeve opening, using the same color you used to start the left sleeve. Place marker and join for working in the round.

Work the rest of the sleeve in the same manner as the left sleeve.

Neck Band

With US 3 [3.25 mm] needles, COLOR 1 and starting at the right shoulder corner, pick up and knit 35 sts along the back neck. Pick up and knit 52 sts along the left front. Pick up 1 st from the angle of the V-neck.

Use a safety pin to mark this stitch, so you can later identify it as the CENTRAL STITCH.

Pick up and knit 52 sts along the right front. Place marker and start working in the round.

Round 1: (K1, p1) to 1 st from central stitch, s2kp (*slip 2 as if to knit 2 together, k1, pass slipped sts over*), (p1, k1) to end of round.

Round 2: Work in ribbing to central st, knit central st, work in ribbing to end of round.

Round 3: K1, (p1, k1) to 1 st from central stitch, s2kp, k1, (p1, k1) to end of round.

Round 4: Work in ribbing to central st, knit central st, work in ribbing to end of round.

Work in the established ribbing for 5 more rounds.

On the next round, BO all sts in pattern.

Finishing

Weave in all ends and block sweater to measurements.

Finished Measurements

Bust circumference (with fronts overlapped and tied): 30 (34, 39, 42½ 46, 49, 55, 58)" [75 (85, 97.5, 106, 115, 122.5, 137.5, 145) cm].

Cross back: 13¼ (14, 15¼, 16, 16¾, 17½, 18½, 19¼)" [33 (35, 38, 40, 42, 44, 46, 48) cm].

Armhole depth: 6½ (6¾, 7½, 7¾, 8, 8½, 8¾, 9¼)" [16 (17, 18.5, 19.5, 20, 21.5, 22, 23) cm].

Upper sleeve circumference: 10½ (11½, 13½, 14½, 15½, 17¼, 18, 19¼)" [26.5 (29, 33.5, 36, 39, 43, 45, 48) cm].

Sleeve length underarm to cuff: 18" [45 cm] or desired length.

Length from underarm to bottom hem: 16 (17, 17, 17, 18, 18, 19, 19)" [35 (37.5, 37.5, 37.5, 40, 40, 42.5, 42.5) cm].

indigo

by veera välimäki

The perfect blue meets cables in this warm everyday sweater! Easy, A-line shaped body and subtle hemline shaping make this sweater lovely to wear. This incredible yarn and color let the cable texture shine. Indigo is the dream sweater for all cable lovers!

indigo

Sizes

XS (S, M, L, XL, 2XL, 3XL). Shown in size S on a 36½" bust.

Finished chest circumference: 36 (40, 44, 48, 52, 56, 60)" [90 (100, 110, 120, 130, 140, 150) cm]. Choose a size with 2-4" [5 to 10 cm] of positive ease.

Materials

Yarn: 6 (7, 8, 8, 9, 9, 10) skeins of Väinämöinen DK by Louhittaren Luola (75% Superwash Wool, 25% Nylon; 206 yds [185 m] / 100 g). Approx. 1220 (1330, 1440, 1530, 1640, 1760, 1880) yds [1110 (1210, 1320, 1400, 1500, 1610, 1720) m] of heavy DK weight yarn. The sample was knit in *Interpretations* special colorway Indigo.

Needles: US 7 [4.5 mm] and US 6 [4 mm] circular needle, 32" [80 cm] long, and dpns in each size. Adjust needle size if necessary to obtain the correct gauge.

Other: Cable needle, stitch markers, stitch holders or waste yarn, tapestry needle and blocking aids. Optional, but highly recommended: row counter.

Gauge

23 sts and 28 rows = 4" [10 cm] in cable pattern, using larger needles.

21 sts and 28 rows = 4" [10 cm] in rev St st, using larger needles.

Finished Measurements

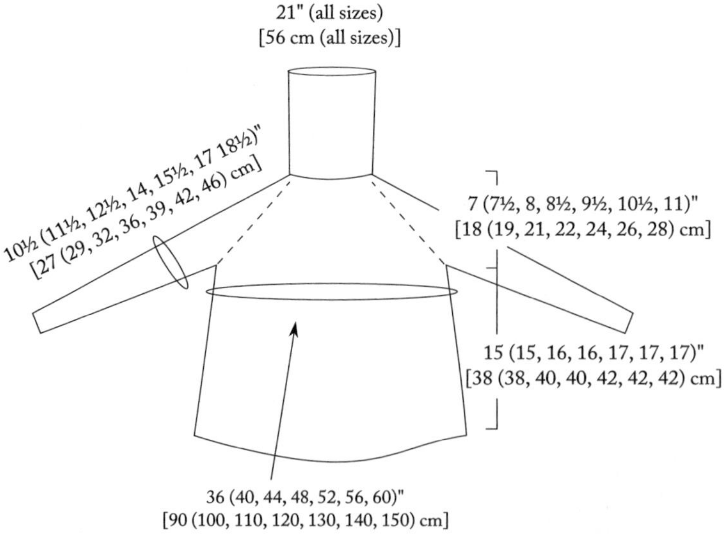

indigo

Collar

Note: All sizes start with the same numbers.

Using smaller circular needle and long-tail cast on, CO 116 sts. Carefully join in round without twisting your stitches and place marker for BOR. Work in 2X2 ribbing (*knit 2, purl 2; repeat from * to end of round) until the collar measures 11" [28 cm].

Yoke

Change to larger circular needle and place markers on next round as follows: Sm, p18 (sleeve), pm, p40 (back), pm, p18 (sleeve), pm, p40 (front stitches) to end of round. Begin yoke increases and cables.

Round 1 (RS): *Sm, m1L, k2, p1, work row 1 of cable A (*see chart for cable A on page 48*), p1, k2, m1R, sm, p1, work row 1 of cable A, p1, m1L (purl), work row 1 of cable A, m1R (purl), p1, work row 1 of cable A, p1; repeat once from *.

Round 2 (RS): *Sm, k3, p1, work the next row of cable A, p1, k3, sm, p1, work the next row of cable A, p2, work the next row of cable A, p2, work the next row of cable A, p1; repeat once from *.

Round 3: *Sm, m1L, k to next purl st, p1, work the next row of cable A, p1, knit to m, m1R, sm, p1, work the next row of cable A, p1, m1L, p1, work the next row of cable A, p1, m1R, p1, work the next row of cable A, p1; repeat once from *.

Round 4: *Sm, k to next purl st, p1, work the next row of cable A, p1, k to m, sm, p1, work the next row of cable A, p1, k1, p1, work the next row of cable A, p1, k1, p1, work the next row of cable A, p1; repeat once from *.

Round 5: *Sm, m1L, k to next purl st, p1, work the next row of cable A, p1, k to m, m1R, sm, p1, work the next row of cable A, p1, m1L, knit to next purl st, p1, work the next row of cable A, p1, k to next purl st, m1R, p1, work the next row of cable A, p1; repeat once from *.

Round 6: *Sm, k to next purl st, p1, work the next row of cable A, p1, k to m, sm, p1, work the next row of cable A, p1, k to next purl st, p1, work the next row of cable A, p1, k to next purl st, p1, work the next row of cable A, p1; repeat once from *.

Repeat ***Rounds 5 and 6*** – 7 more times ***and at the same time*** start working cable A with the increased knit-stitches when you have enough stitches for a half repeat (6 sts; note that cables are always twisting in opposite direction). *80 stitches increased; you should have 196 stitches on needles.*

Round 7 (RS, sleeve and body increases): *Sm, m1L (purl), work the next row of cable A, p1, work the next row of cable A, p1, work the next row of cable A, m1R (purl), sm, p1, work the next row of cable A, p1, m1L, k3, C6B, p1, work the next row of cable A, p1, C6F, k3, m1R, p1, work the next row of cable A, p1; repeat once from *.

Round 8 (RS): *Sm, p1, [work the next row of cable A, p1] three times, sm, p1, work the next row of cable A, p1, k to next purl st, p1, work the next row of cable A, p1, k to m, p1, work the next row of cable A, p1; repeat once from *.

Round 9 (body increases): *Sm, p1, [work the next row of cable A, p1] three times, sm, p1, work the next row of cable A, p1, m1L, knit to next purl st (10), p1, work the next row of cable A, p1, k to next purl st (10), m1R, p1, work the next row of cable A, p1; repeat once from *.

Round 10: *Sm, p1, [work the next row of cable A, p1] three times, sm, p1, work the next row of cable A, p1, k to next purl st, p1, work the next row of cable A, p1, k to next purl st, p1, work the next row of cable A, p1; repeat once from *.

Round 11 (sleeve and body increases): *Sm, m1L (purl), p to next cable, [work the next row of cable A, p1] three times, p to m, m1R (purl), sm, p1, work the next row of cable A, p1, m1L, knit to next purl st (11), p1, work the next row of cable A, p1, k to next purl st (11), m1R, p1, work the next row of cable A, p1; repeat once from *.

Round 12: *Sm, p to next cable, [work the next row of cable A, p1] three times, p to m, sm, p1, work the next row of cable A, p1, k to next purl st, p1, work the next row of cable A, p1, k to next purl st, p1, work the next row of cable A, p1; repeat once from *.

Round 13 (body increases): *Sm, p to next cable, [work the next row of cable A, p1] three times, p to m, sm, p1, work the next row of cable A, p1, m1L (purl), work the same row of chart A as for the other repeats for the next 12 sts, p1, work the next row of cable A, p1, work the same row of chart A as for the other repeats for the next 12 sts, m1R (purl), p1, work the next row of cable A, p1; repeat once from *.

Round 14: *Sm, p to next cable, [work the next row of cable A, p1] three times, p to m, sm, p1, work the next row of cable A, p2, [work the next row of cable A, p1] three times, p1, work the next row of cable A, p1; repeat once from *.

Round 15 (sleeve and body increases): *Sm, m1L (purl), p to next cable, [work the next row of cable A, p1] three times, p to m, m1R (purl), sm, p1, work the next row of cable A, p1, m1L, p1, [work the next row of cable A, p1] three times, m1R, p1, work the next row of cable A, p1; repeat once from *.

Round 16: *Sm, p to next cable, [work the next row of cable A, p1] three times, p to m, sm, p1, work the next row of cable A, p1, k to next purl st, p1, [work the next row of cable A, p1] three times, k to next purl st, p1, work the next row of cable A, p1; repeat once from *.

Round 17 (body increases): *Sm, purl to next cable, [work the next row of cable A, p1] three times, p to m, sm, p1, work the next row of cable A, p1, m1L, k to next purl st, p1, [work the next row of cable A, p1] three times, k to next purl st, m1R, p1, work the next row of cable A, p1; repeat once from *.

Round 18: *Sm, p to next cable, [work the next row of cable A, p1] three times, p to m, sm, p1, work the next row of cable A, p1, k to next purl st, p1, [work the next row of cable A, p1] three times, k to next purl st, p1, work the next row of cable A, p1; repeat once from *.

Round 19 (sleeve and body increases): *Sm, m1L (purl), purl to next cable, [work the next row of cable A, p1] three times, p to m, m1R (purl), sm, p1, work the next row of cable A, p1, m1L, knit to next purl st, p1, [work the next row of cable A, p1] three times, k to next purl st, m1R, p1, work the next row of cable A, p1; repeat once from *.

Round 20: *Sm, p to next cable, [work the next row of cable A, p1] three times, p to m, sm, p1, work the next row of cable A, p1, k to next purl st, p1, [work the next row of cable A, p1] three times, k to next purl st, p1, work the next row of cable A, p1; repeat once from *.

Round 21 (body increases): *Sm, purl to next cable, [work the next row of cable A, p1] three times, p to m, sm, p1, work the next row of cable A, p1, m1L, k to next purl st, p1, [work the next row of cable A, p1] three times, k to next purl st, m1R, p1, work the next row of cable A, p1; repeat once from *.

Round 22 (RS): *Sm, p to next cable, [work the next row of cable A, p1] three times, p to m, sm, p1, work the next row of cable A, p1, k to next purl st, p1, [work the next row of cable A, p1] three times, k to next purl st, p1, work the next row of cable A, p1; repeat once from *.

Repeat ***Rounds 19-22*** – 4 more times. *You should now have 292 sts on needle.*

Round 23 (RS, sleeve and body increases): *Sm, m1L (purl), purl to next cable, [work the next row of cable A, p1] three times, p to m, m1R (purl), sm, p1, work the next row of cable A, p1, m1L (purl), [work the next row of cable A, p1] four times, work the next row of cable A, m1R (purl), p1, work the next row of cable A, p1; repeat once from *.

Round 24: *Sm, p to next cable, [work the next row of cable A, p1] three times, p to m, sm, p1, work the next row of cable A, p to cable, [work the next row of cable A, p1] five times, p1, work the next row of cable A, p1; repeat once from *.

Round 25 (body increases): *Sm, purl to next cable, [work the next row of cable A, p1] three times, p to m, sm, p1, work the next row of cable A, p1, m1L (purl), p1, [work the next row of cable A, p1] five times, m1R (purl), p1, work the next row of cable A, p1; repeat once from *.

Round 26: *Sm, p to next cable, [work the next row of cable A, p1] three times, p to m, sm, p1, work the next row of cable A, p to cable, [work the next row of cable A, p1] five times, p to cable, work the next row of cable A, p1; repeat once from *.

Round 27 (sleeve and body increases): *Sm, m1L (purl), purl to next cable, [work the next row of cable A, p1] three times, p to m, m1R (purl), sm, p1, work the next row of cable A, p1, m1L (purl), p to cable, [work the next row of cable A, p1] five times, p to 1 st before next cable, m1R (purl), p1, work the next row of cable A, p1; repeat once from *.

Round 28: *Sm, p to next cable, [work the next row of cable A, p1] three times, p to m, sm, p1, work the next row of cable A, p to cable, [work the next row of cable A, p1] five times, p to cable, work the next row of cable A, p1; repeat once from *.

Round 29 (body increases): *Sm, p to next cable, [work the next row of cable A, p1] three times, p to m, sm, p1, work the next row of cable A, p1, m1L (purl), p to cable, [work the next row of cable A, p1] five times, p to 1 st before next cable, m1R (purl), p1, work the next row of cable A, p1; repeat once from *.

Round 30: *Sm, p to next cable, [work the next row of cable A, p1] three times, p to m, sm, p1, work the next row of cable A, p to cable, [work the next row of cable A, p1] five times, p to cable, work the next row of cable A, p1; repeat once from *.

Repeat ***Rounds 27-30*** – 0 (2, 5, 7, 9, 12, 15) times more. *You should have 316 (340, 376, 400, 424, 460, 496) sts on needle. Note: Make a note of the row you have just completed of chart A, as you will need this info when knitting 'Sleeves' later.*

Divide for body and sleeves

Next round (RS): *Remove marker, place the stitches before next marker on holder for sleeve, CO 0 (1, 1, 2, 3, 4, 4) sts, pm (this is new BOR), CO 0 (1, 1, 2, 3, 4, 4) sts, remove marker, p1, work the next row of cable A, p to cable, [work the next row of cable A, p1] five times, p to cable, work the next row of cable A, p1; repeat once from *

You should have 200 (220, 244, 264, 284, 312, 336) sts on needle for body and 58 (62, 68, 72, 76, 82, 88) sts on each holder for sleeves.

Body

Continue with body stitches on needle. Work 2" [5 cm] even in cable pattern as established: *Sm, p to cable, work the next row of cable A, p to cable, [work the next row of cable A, p1] five times, purl to cable, work the next row of cable A, p to m; repeat once from *.

Begin A-line shaping.

Increase round (RS): *Sm, p to cable, work the next row of cable A, m1L (purl), p to cable, [work the next row of cable A, p1] five times, p to cable, m1R (purl), work the next row of cable A, p to m; repeat once from *.

Repeat the ***Increase Round*** 7 more times every 8th round. Continue even until the body measures 12 (12, 13, 13, 14, 14, 14)" [32 (32, 34, 34, 36, 36, 36) cm] from underarm. Shape the hem with short rows as follows. *Note: start short rows on an odd row of chart A.*

Short row 1 (RS): Sm, p to cable, work the next row of cable A, p to cable, [work the next row of cable A, p1] five times, p to last purl stitch before next cable, W&T.

Short Row 2 (WS): K to cable, [purl the cable sts, k1] five times, k to last st before next cable, W&T.

Short Row 3 (RS): P to cable, [work the next row of cable A, p1] five times, p to last purl stitch before previous wrapped st, W&T.

Short Row 4 (WS): K to cable, [purl the cable sts, k1] five times, k to last st before previous wrapped st, W&T.

Repeat ***Short Rows 3 and 4*** – 4 more times. Work over to front side on next row (RS): Purl to cable, [work the next row of cable A, p1] five times, purl to first wrapped st, *p2tog the wrap with the wrapped st, m1R (purl); repeat from * until all wraps from this set have been picked up, work the next row of cable A, p to side marker.

Continue on RS and work the Short Rows similarly on the front side.

Short row 1 (RS): Sm, p to cable, work the next row of cable A, p to cable, [work the next row of cable A, p1] five times, p to last purl stitch before next cable, W&T.

Short Row 2 (WS): K to cable, [purl the cable sts, k1] five times, k to last st before next cable, W&T.

Short Row 3 (RS): P to cable, [work the next row of cable A, p1] five times, p to last purl stitch before previous wrapped st, W&T.

Short Row 4 (WS): K to cable, [purl the cable sts, k1] five times, k to last st before previous wrapped st, W&T.

Repeat ***Short Rows 3 and 4*** – 4 more times. Work over to BOR on next row (RS): P to cable, [work the next row of cable A, p1] five times, p to first wrapped st, *p2tog the wrap with the wrapped st, m1R (purl); repeat from * until all wraps from this set have been picked up, work the next row of cable A, p to side marker.

Pick up remaining wrap-sets on next round (RS): *Sm, p to cable, work the next row of cable A, *ssp the wrap with the wrapped st, m1L (purl); repeat from * until all wraps from this set have been picked up [work the next row of cable A, p1] five times, p to cable, work the next row of cable A, p to m; repeat once from *.

Change to smaller circular needle and work 1¾" [4 cm] 2X2 ribbing. *Note: if your stitches are not dividable by 4, decrease needed stitches at each side.* BO sts in ribbing.

Sleeves

Place 58 (62, 68, 72, 76, 82, 88) sleeve sts on larger dpns. Attach yarn to centre of the underarm / centre of underarm CO stitches and pick up and knit 0 (1, 1, 3, 5, 6, 7) sts to stitches on needles, work the sleeve sts in pattern as established, pick up and knit 0 (1, 1, 3, 5, 6, 7) sts to centre of underarm. *You should have 58 (64, 70, 78, 86, 94, 102) stitches on needle.* Place marker to indicate the BOR. *Note: You will pick up more stitches than you cast-on for the body for some sizes; do not decrease any of these stitches.*

Work in rev St st and cable patterns as established until the sleeve measures 2" [5 cm] from underarm as follows -

Round 1 (RS): Sm, p to next cable, [work the next row of cable A, p1] three times, p to m.

Begin decreases.

Decrease Round (RS): Sm, p2, ssp, work to last 4 sts as established in rev St st and cable patterns, p2tog, p2.

Repeat ***Decrease Round*** every 1¼" [3 cm] for 6 (7, 8, 8, 10, 10) more times. *You should have 44 (48, 52, 60, 68, 72, 80) stitches on needle.* Continue even until the sleeve measures 18" [45 cm] from underarm.

Change to smaller dpns and work 3" [8 cm] in 2X2 ribbing. BO sleeve stitches in pattern.

Finishing

Weave in all yarn ends and block the sweater lightly using your preferred method.

Cable A

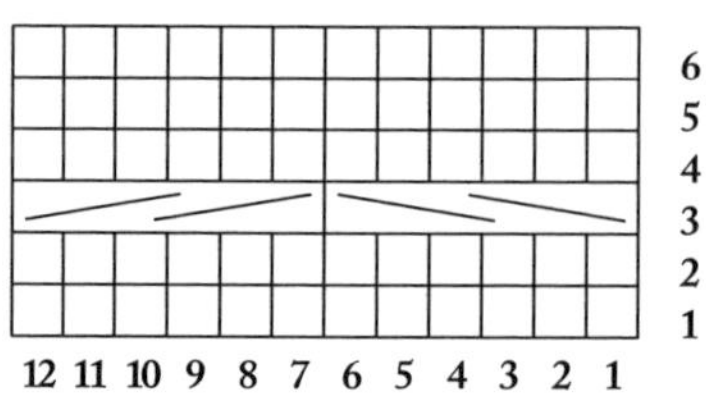

St st; knit on RS, purl on WS

C6F

C6B

shelter

You have given me promises of shelter, a safe haven to raise our children with unconditional love and peace.

A warm light forever shines from within our home welcoming neighbors and those that may be in need. Never will those with bad intentions break through our fortified place because only we hold the keys.

Forever locked in your arms, you are my umbrella shielding me from the weight my outside life brings. Our paradise is my retreat, where I always long to be.

When the days go sour, the thought of home puts a smile back on my face. Racing back to my hideaway, to you, shaded from the influences of the world.

Our children have outgrown their cradles, and will one day soon leave our sanctuary. They will trade us for adventure, bargaining safety for exploration. Our fortress will still be there standing in anticipation of their return.

If our palace ever burns, if our walls come crashing to the ground, I will not worry for a house is not a home. It is you that gives my heart shelter, in you I find my peace. With you I can live anywhere because only you provide me my relief.

shelter

tree seeker wrap

rose quartz cardigan

tree seeker

by joji locatelli

Big scarves and wraps are the perfect blank canvas to play with your favorite stitch patterns. For this design I chose a beautiful interlocking cable and a delicate lace pattern that compliment each other perfectly.

I picked a beautiful cashmere yarn for this design that makes it irresistible. I may never take this off...

free seeker

Sizes

ONE SIZE

Finished measurements: 22½" [56 cm] wide and 75" [188 cm] long. *See schematic below.*

Materials

Yarn: 7 skeins of Bello Worsted by The Plucky Knitter (55% Merino/45% Cashmere; 200 yds [183 m] / 105 g) or approx. 1300 yds [1190 m] of light worsted weight yarn. The sample was made using *Interpretations* special colorway Pewter.

Needles: US 7 [4.5 mm] straight or circular needles, at least 24" [60 cm] long.

Other: Stitch markers, cable needle, tapestry needle.

Gauge

19 sts and 28 rows = 4" [10 cm] in Stockinette St (for reference) on US 7 [4.5 mm] needles.

One Cable repeat measures 3¼" [8 cm] wide and 2½" [6 cm] tall, worked in US 7 [4.5 mm] needles.

Before you measure, please take the time to wash and block your swatch in the same manner that you will wash and block your wrap.

Finished Measurements

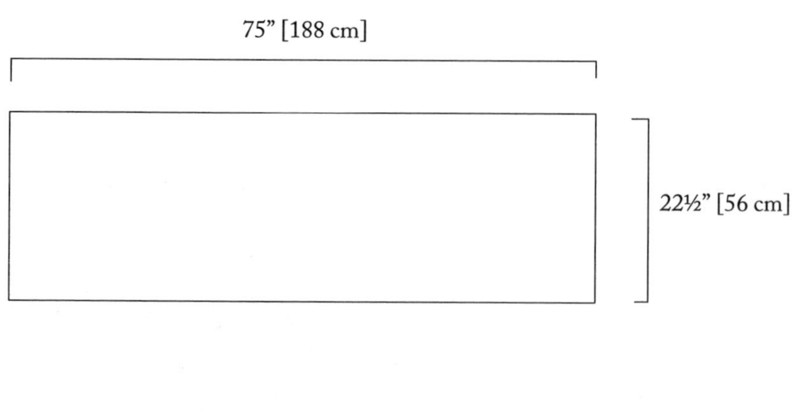

tree seeker

Beginning

CO 95 sts.

Row 1: P1, (ktbl, p1) to end of row.

Row 2: K1, (ptbl, k1) to end of row.

Repeat the last 2 rows 4 more times.

Next row: Same as row 1.

Next row: K1, (ptbl, k1) twice, pm, *p4, m1L (purl), p4, m1L (purl), p4, m1L (purl), p5, pm, k1, ptbl, k1, p11, k1, ptbl, k1, pm*, repeat from * once more, p4, m1L (purl), p4, m1L (purl), p4, m1L (purl), p5, pm, k1, (ptbl, k1) twice.

You should have 108 sts.

Body

Find Cable and Lace charts on page 56 and written instructions for these panels on page 57. All of them are 16 row repeats.

Row 1 (RS): P1, (ktbl, p1) twice, sm, work row 1 of CABLE, sm, row 1 of LACE A, work row 1 of CABLE, sm, row 1 of LACE B, sm, work row 1 of CABLE, sm, p1, (ktbl, p1) twice.

Row 2 (WS): K1, (ptbl, k1) twice, sm, work foll row of CABLE, sm, work foll row of LACE B, sm, work foll row of CABLE, sm, work foll row of LACE A, sm, work foll row of CABLE, sm, k1, (ptbl, k1) to end of row.

Work in this manner, always working the following row of the cable and lace panels until work measures approx. 70" [175 cm], ending with row 2 of the repeat.

Ending

Next row (RS): P1, (ktbl, p1) twice, *remove m, ssk, k4, ssk, k5, k2tog, k5, remove m, p1, ktbl, p1, k4, ssk, k5, k2tog, p1, ktbl, p1*, repeat from * once, remove m, ssk, k4, ssk, k5, k2tog, k5, remove m, p1, (ktbl, p1) twice.

Next row (WS): K1, (ptbl, k1) to end of row.

Net row (RS): P1, (ktbl, p1) to end of row.

Work 7 more rows in the established ribbing and on the foll row BO all sts loosely in pattern

Finishing

Weave in all ends and block wrap to measurements.

Charts for the lace and Cable patterns

LACE A

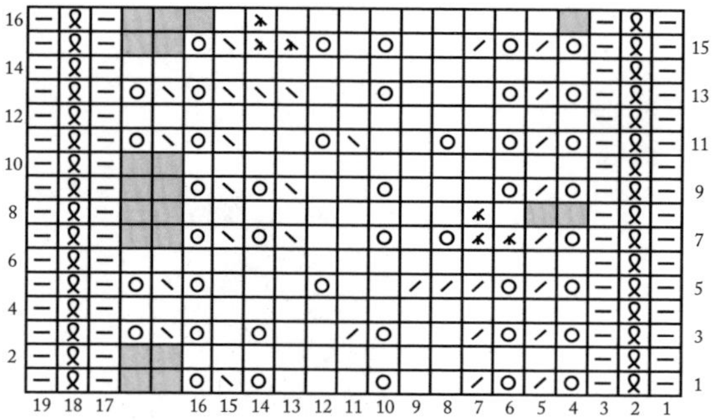

LACE B

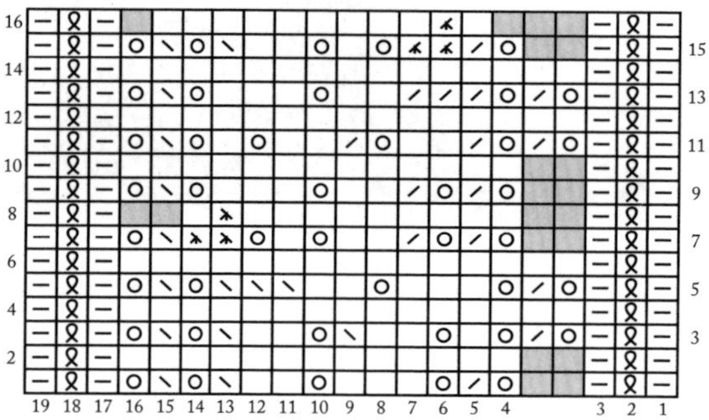

CABLE

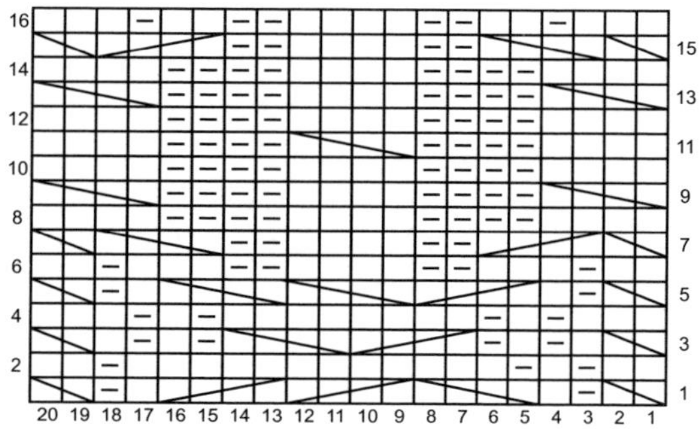

Knit on the RS, purl on the WS

Purl on the RS, knit on the WS

Left Twist: see Glossary

C4B (slip 2 onto cable needle and hold in back, k2, k2 from CN)

C4F (slip 2 onto cable needle and hold in front, k2, k2 from CN)

Knit through the back loop on the RS, purl through the back loop on the WS

Yo (yarn over)

K2tog (knit 2 together) on the RS, p2tog (purl 2 together on the WS)

Ssk (slip, slip, knit) on the RS,
p2tog tbl (purl 2 together through the back loop) on the WS

K3tog (knit 3 together) on the RS, p3tog (purl 3 together on the WS)

Sssk (slip, slip, slip, knit) on the RS,
p3tog tbl (purl 3 together through the back loop) on the WS

No stitch

Written Instructions

Cable

Row 1: Left Twist (*LT - see Glossary)*, p1, k1, C4F, C4B, C4B, k1, p1, LT.

Row 2: P2, k1, p12, k1, p1, k1, p2.

Row 3: LT, k1, p1, k1, p1, C4B, C4F, p1, k1, p1, k1, LT.

Row 4: P3, k1, p1, k1, p8, k1, p1, k1, p3.

Row 5: LT, p1, k1, C4B, C4F, C4F, k1, p1, LT.

Row 6: P2, k1, p3, k2, p4, k2, p3, k1, p2.

Row 7: LT, C4B, p2, k4, p2, C4F, LT.

Rows 8, 10, 12, 14: P4, k4, p4, k4, p4.

Row 9: C4F, p4, k4, p4, C4F.

Row 11: K4, p4, C4F, p4, k4.

Row 13: C4F, p4, k4, p4, C4F.

Row 15: LT, C4F, p2, k4, p2, C4B, LT.

Row 16: P3, k1, p2, k2, p4, k2, p2, k1, p3.

Lace A

Row 1: P1, ktbl, p1, yo, k2tog, yo, k2tog, k2, yo, k3, yo, ssk, yo, p1, ktbl, p1.

Row 2: K1, ptbl, k1, p13, k1, ptbl, k1.

Row 3: P1, ktbl, p1, yo, k2tog, yo, k2tog, k2, yo, k2tog, k2, yo, k1, yo, ssk, yo, p1, ktbl, p1.

Row 4: K1, ptbl, k1, p15, k1, ptbl, k1.

Row 5: P1, ktbl, p1, yo, k2tog, yo, k2tog, k2tog, k2tog, k2, yo, k3, yo, ssk, yo, p1, ktbl, p1.

Row 6: K1, ptbl, k1, p15, k1, ptbl, k1.

Row 7: P1, ktbl, p1, yo, k2tog, k3tog, k3tog, yo, k1, yo, k2, ssk, yo, ssk, yo, p1, ktbl, p1.

Row 8: K1, ptbl, k1, p9, p3tog, p1, k1, ptbl, k1.

Row 9: P1, ktbl, p1, yo, k2tog, yo, k3, yo, k2, ssk, yo, ssk, yo, p1, ktbl, p1.

Row 10: K1, ptbl, k1, p13, k1, ptbl, k1.

Row 11: P1, ktbl, p1, yo, k2tog, yo, k1, yo, k2, ssk, yo, k2, ssk, yo, ssk, yo, p1, ktbl, p1.

Row 12: K1, ptbl, k1, p15, k1, ptbl, k1.

Row 13: P1, ktbl, p1, yo, k2tog, yo, k3, yo, k2, ssk, ssk, ssk, yo, ssk, yo, p1, ktbl, p1.

Row 14: K1, ptbl, k1, p15, k1, ptbl, k1.

Row 15: P1, ktbl, p1, yo, k2tog, yo, k2tog, k2, yo, k1, yo, sssk, sssk, ssk, yo, p1, ktbl, p1.

Row 16: K1, ptbl, k1, p1, p3tog tbl, p9, k1, ptbl, k1.

Lace B

Row 1: P1, ktbl, p1, yo, k2tog, yo, k3, yo, k2, ssk, yo, ssk, yo, p1, ktbl, p1.

Row 2: K1, ptbl, k1, p13, k1, ptbl, k1.

Row 3: P1, ktbl, p1, yo, k2tog, yo, k1, yo, k2, ssk, yo, k2, ssk, yo, ssk, yo, p1, ktbl, p1.

Row 4: K1, ptbl, k1, p15, k1, ptbl, k1.

Row 5: P1, ktbl, p1, yo, k2tog, yo, k3, yo, k2, ssk, ssk, ssk, yo, ssk, yo, p1, ktbl, p1.

Row 6: K1, ptbl, k1, p15, k1, ptbl, k1.

Row 7: P1, ktbl, p1, yo, k2tog, yo, k2tog, k2, yo, k1, yo, sssk, sssk, ssk, yo, p1, ktbl, p1.

Row 8: K1, ptbl, k1, p1, p3tog tbl, p9, k1, ptbl, k1.

Row 9: P1, ktbl, p1, yo, k2tog, yo, k2tog, k2, yo, k3, yo, ssk, yo, p1, ktbl, p1.

Row 10: K1, ptbl, k1, p13, k1, ptbl, k1.

Row 11: P1, ktbl, p1, yo, k2tog, yo, k2tog, k2, yo, k2tog, k2, yo, k1, yo, ssk, yo, p1, ktbl, p1.

Row 12: K1, ptbl, k1, p15, k1, ptbl, k1.

Row 13: P1, ktbl, p1, yo, k2tog, yo, k2tog, k2tog, k2tog, k2, yo, k3, yo, ssk, yo, p1, ktbl, p1.

Row 14: K1, ptbl, k1, p15, k1, ptbl, k1.

Row 15: P1, ktbl, p1, yo, k2tog, k3tog, k3tog, yo, k1, yo, k2, ssk, yo, ssk, yo, p1, ktbl, p1.

Row 16: K1, ptbl, k1, p9, p3tog, p1, k1, ptbl, k1.

rose quartz

by veera välimaki

This lovely layering piece keeps you sheltered and safe throughout the changing of seasons! This open front cardigan is worked from top down in one piece and all the small details like long garter stitch cuffs and deep pockets are designed for ultimate comfort. Sweet blush pink color takes this cardigan up a notch making it classy and fun to knit.

rose quartz

Sizes

XS (S, M, L, XL, 2XL). Shown in size M on a 36½" bust.

Finished width of the back: 16 (18, 20, 22, 24, 26)" [40 (45, 50, 55, 60, 65) cm]. Choose a size with approx. 2" [5 cm] of positive ease.

Materials

Yarn: 6 (6, 7, 8, 9, 10) skeins of House DK by House of A La Mode (100% Merino Wool; 250 yds [195 m] / 115 g). Approx. 1170 (1280, 1450, 1640, 1780, 1920) yds [1070 (1170, 1330, 1500, 1630, 1760) m] of DK weight yarn. The sample was knit in *Interpretations* special colorway Kissed Quartz.

Needles: US 8 [5 mm] and US 6 [4 mm] circular needle, 32" [80 cm] long or longer, and dpns. Adjust needle size if necessary to obtain the correct gauge.

Other: Stitch markers, stitch holders or waste yarn, tapestry needle and blocking aids.

Gauge

18 sts and 26 rows = 4" [10 cm] in Stockinette stitch using larger needles.

Finished Measurements

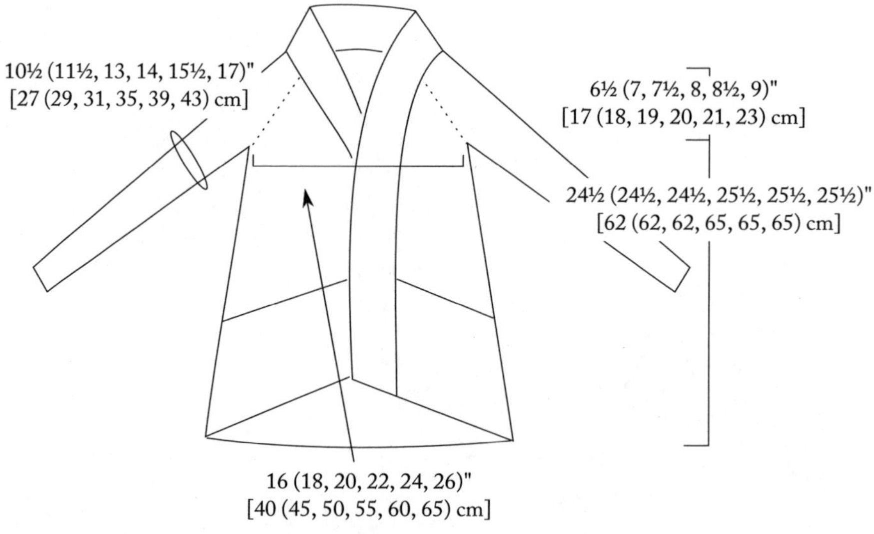

rose quartz

Yoke

Using larger circular needle, CO 64 (66, 66, 68, 72, 72) stitches using a long-tail cast-on. Do not join. Knit the first row (WS). Begin yoke shaping as follows:

Row 1 (RS): K3, m1L, knit 16 (16, 16, 18, 20, 20), m1R, k3, pm, m1L, knit 20 (22, 22, 20, 20, 20), m1R, pm, k3, m1L, knit 16 (16, 16, 18, 20, 20), m1R, k3 to end.

Row 2 (WS): Purl to m, sm, m1R (purl), purl to marker, m1L (purl), sm, purl to end.

Row 3 (RS): K3, m1L, knit to 3 sts before marker, m1R, k3, sm, m1R, knit to marker, m1L, sm, k3, m1L, knit to 3 sts before marker, m1R, k3 to end.

Row 4 (WS): Purl to m, sm, m1L (purl), purl to marker, m1R (purl), sm, purl to end.

Repeat ***Rows 3 and 4*** – 11 (13, 15, 18, 20, 23) more times. Cut yarn. *You should have 168 (186, 202, 228, 248, 272) sts on needle.*

Divide for body and sleeves

Next row (RS): Starting from the left end of the CO-edge, re-attach yarn and pick up and knit 26 (30, 34, 40, 44, 50) stitches down along the left front to the stitches on needle, place the stitches before marker on holder for sleeve, sm, knit the back stitches, sm, place the remaining stitches on another holder for second sleeve and pick up and knit 26 (30, 34, 40, 44, 50) stitches up along the right front to corner of CO-edge.

You should have 48 (52, 56, 64, 70, 76) sts on each holder for the sleeves and 124 (142, 158, 180, 196, 220) sts on needle for the body.

Body

Continue working the body stitches on needle in St st with yarn attached. Work 5 rows and then begin increases as follows.

Increase Row (RS): Knit to m, m1R, sm, knit to m, sm, m1L, knit to end.

Repeat ***Increase Row*** every 4th row (*every second RS row*). Continue as established until the body measures 16 (16, 16, 17, 17, 17)" [40 (40, 40, 43, 43, 43) cm] from underarm.

On next ***Increase Row***, place pockets as follows: Knit to 35 stitches before marker, place the next 25 on holder/waste yarn for pocket lining, cast on 25 sts using backwards loop CO, knit to m, m1R, sm, knit to m, sm, m1L, k10, place the next 25 on holder/waste yarn for pocket lining, cast on 25 sts using backwards loop CO, knit to end.

Continue in garter st (*knit on RS and WS*) and at the same time repeat Increase Row every 4th row (*every second RS row*) 9 more times. After all increases, continue in garter st until the body measures 24½ (24½, 24½, 25½, 25½, 25½)" [62 (62, 62, 65, 65, 65) cm] from underarm.

BO body stitches on next RS row.

Sleeves

Place the held 48 (52, 56, 64, 70, 76) stitches on larger dpns. Attach yarn to underarm, join in round and place a BOR marker. Work 2" [5 cm] in St st. Begin decreases:

Decrease Round (RS): K2, ssk, knit to last 4 sts, k2tog, k2.

Repeat ***Decrease Round*** every 1¾" [4 cm] for 6 (6, 7, 8, 9, 10) more times. *You should have 34 (38, 40, 46, 50, 54) stitches on needles.* Continue even until the sleeve measures 18" [45 cm] from underarm.

Change to smaller dpns and work 3" [8 cm] in garter st. BO sleeve stitches on next knit round.

Collar and Front Bands

Using smaller circular needle and with RS of the sweater facing, starting from the hem corner, pick up and knit 68 (69, 71, 73, 75, 75) stitches up the right front to the CO edge, pick up and knit 64 (66, 66, 68, 72, 72) stitches from the CO-edge and pick up and knit 68 (69, 71, 73, 75, 75) stitches down the left front. *You should have 200 (204, 208, 214, 222, 222) stitches on needle.*

Knit the next row (WS) and place a marker in the center of the back, after 100 (102, 104, 107, 111, 111) stitches.

Begin short row shaping as follows. *Note: There's no need to pick up the wraps as they will blend in garter stitch nicely.*

Row 5 (RS): Knit to 10 sts before marker, m1R, k to m, sm, k10, m1L, k2, W&T.

Row 6 (WS): Knit to m, sm, knit 12, W&T.

Row 7 (RS): Knit to 10 sts before marker, m1R, k to m, sm, k10, m1L, knit to previous wrapped st, k3 (two sts after the previous wrapped st), W&T.

Row 8 (WS): Knit to m, sm, knit to previous wrapped st, k3 (two sts after the previous wrapped st), W&T.

Repeat ***Rows 7 and 8*** – 13 more times. *You should have 230 (234, 238, 244, 252, 252) stitches on needle.* Continue even in garter stitch (*no more increases or short rows*), until the front bands measure 5" [12 cm]. BO all sts on next RS row.

Pocket linings

Place the held pocket lining stitches on larger needles and attach yarn. Increase on first row (RS): K1, m1R, knit to last stitch, m1L, k1. Work 5" [12 cm] in St st and BO lining stitches on next row.

Finishing

Seam the pocket linings on WS. Weave in all yarn ends and block the sweater lightly using your preferred method.

movement

Elevate yourself beyond the flatness of regularity. Open your mind and break new ground by taking your first steps toward a new reality that you create.

Study your thoughts and allow the movement of your synapses to spin around like dragonflies, chasing life over still waters.

As you pick up your needles and catch your flow, counting stitches to your own special rhythm, feel the happiness course through you to the tips of your fingers and toes.

That rhythm can take you to a place where new discoveries can be made, where your happiness can pour out. A place where sadness will eventually dissipate and fearfulness can be massaged away.

Ride high on the crest of your new existence. In that place where the ocean meets the shore, where needle meets wool, where emotions can be diverted even if only for just a while.

Go. Discover where your inertia lies and move yourself to bring forth some satisfaction.

movement

dynamic trio shawl

anemone top

dynamic trio

by joji locatelli

One, two, three colors dance together to the rhythm of this shawl creating a beautiful flowing sequence of stripes.

Increases, decreases, yarnovers and garter, all playing together to create this stunning piece.

dynamic trio

Sizes

ONE SIZE

Finished measurements: 80" [200 cm] long and 40" [100 cm] deep at deepest point. *See schematic below.*

Materials

Yarn: 3 skeins of Top Draw Sock by Skein (85% Merino, 15% Nylon; 437 yds [400 m] / 95g) in 3 different colors. You will need approx. 385 yds [350 m] of Color 1; 330 yds [300 m] of Color 2 and 385 yds [350 m] of Color 3. The sample was made using colorways Sway (pale blue speckled), Flight (blue purple) and Tango (coral).

Needles: US 4 [3.5 mm] straight or circular needles, at least 24" [60 cm] long.

Other: Stitch markers, cable needle, tapestry needle.

Gauge

18 sts and 38 rows = 4" [10 cm] in Garter St on US 4 [3.5 mm] needles.

Before you measure, please take the time to wash and block your swatch in the same manner that you will wash and block your shawl.

Finished Measurements

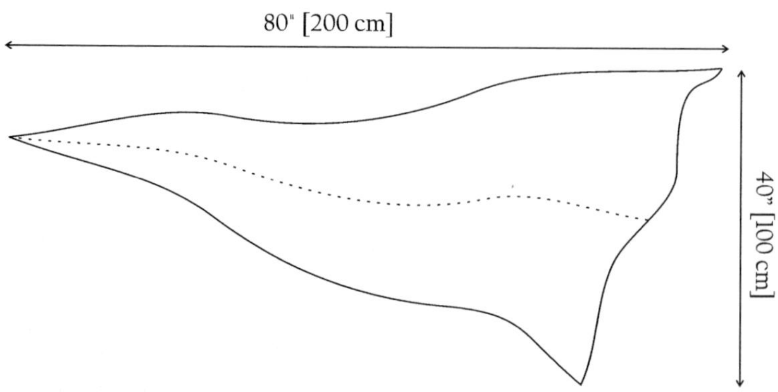

dynamic trio

Movement 1

With Color 1, cast on 8 sts

Row 1: K2, pm, k2, pm, k2, pm, k2.

Row 2 and all foll even-numbered rows: K to end.

Row 3: *K1, m1R, k1, sm, k1, m1L, k1*, sm, repeat from * to *. *12 sts.*

Row 5: K to end.

Row 7: *K2, m1R, k1, sm, k1, m1L, k2*, sm, repeat from * to *. *16 sts.*

Row 9: *K2tog, k1, m1R, k1, sm, k1, m1L, k1, ssk*, sm, repeat from * to *.

Row 11: K to end.

Row 13: K to 1 st from m, m1R, k1, sm, k1, m1L, k to m, sm, k to 1 st from m, m1R, k1, sm, k1, m1L, k to end. *4 sts increased.*

Row 15: K2tog, k to 1 st from m, m1R, k1, sm, k1, m1L, k to 2 sts from m, ssk, sm, k2tog, k to 1 st from m, m1R, k1, sm, k1, m1L, k to 2 sts from end, ssk.

Row 16: K to end.

Rows 17-20: Work rows 15-16 twice.

Rows 21-108: Repeat Rows 13-20 11 more times. *64 sts.*

Movement 2

Row 1: Change to Color 2. K to 1 st from m, m1R, k1, sm, k1, m1L, k to m, sm, k to 1 st from m, m1R, k1, sm, k1, m1L, k to end. *4 sts increased.*

Row 2 and all foll WS rows: K to end.

Row 3: Change to Color 1. K2tog, k to 1 st from m, m1R, k1, sm, k1, m1L, k to 2 sts from m, ssk, sm, k2tog, k to 1 st from m, m1R, k1, sm, k1, m1L, k to 2 sts from end, ssk.

Row 5: Change to Color 2 and repeat row 3.

Row 7: Change to Color 1. K2tog, k to 1 st from m, m1R, k1, sm, k1, m1L, k to m, sm, k2tog, k to 1 st from m, m1R, k1, sm, k1, m1L, k to end. *2 sts increased.*

Row 9: Same as row 5.

Row 11: Same as row 3.

Work Row 12 as all the other WS rows.

Repeat ***Rows 1-12*** 9 more times. *124 sts.*

Movement 3

Row 1: Change to Color 3. K to 1 st from m, m1R, k1, sm, k1, m1L, k to m, sm, K to 1 st from m, m1R, k1, sm, k1, m1L, k to end. *4 sts increased.*

Row 2 and all foll WS rows: K to end.

Row 3: Change to Color 1. K2tog, k to 1 st from m, m1R, k1, sm, k1, m1L, k to 2 sts from m, ssk, sm, k2tog, k to 1 st from m, m1R, k1, sm, k1, m1L, k to 2 sts from end, ssk.

Row 5: Change to Color 2. K2tog, k to 1 st from m, m1R, k1, sm, k1, m1L, k to 2 sts from m, ssk, sm, k2tog, k to 1 st from m, m1R, k1, sm, k1, m1L, k to 2 sts from end, ssk.

Row 7: Change to Color 3. K to 1 st from m, m1R, k1, sm, k1, m1L, k to 2 sts from m, ssk, sm, k to 1 st from m, m1R, k1, sm, k1, m1L, k to 2 sts from end, ssk. *2 sts increased.*

Row 9: Same as row 3.

Row 11: Same as row 5.

Work Row 12 as all the other WS rows.

Repeat ***Rows 1-12*** 9 more times. *184 sts.* Break yarns Color 1 and 2.

Movement 4

Row 1: Change to Color 3. K to 1 st from m, m1R, k1, sm, k1, m1L, k to m, sm, K to 1 st from m, m1R, k1, sm, k1, m1L, k to end. *4 sts increased.*

Row 2: K to end.

Row 3: K2tog, (yo, ssk) to 1 st from m, m1R, k1, sm, k1, m1L, (k2tog, yo) to 2 sts from m, ssk, sm, k2tog, (yo, ssk) to 1 st from m, m1R, k1, sm, k1, m1L, (k2tog, yo) to 2 sts from end, ssk.

Row 4: K to end.

Rows 5-8: Work Rows 3-4 twice.

Row 9: K2, (yo, ssk) to 1 st from m, m1R, k1, sm, k1, m1L, (k2tog, yo) to 2 sts from m, k2, sm, k2, (yo, ssk) to 1 st from m, m1R, k1, sm, k1, m1L, (k2tog, yo) to 2 sts from end, k2. *4 sts increased.*

Row 10: K to end.

Row 11: K2tog, k1, (yo, ssk) to 1 st from m, m1R, k1, sm, k1, m1L, (k2tog, yo) to 3 sts from m, k1, ssk, sm, k2tog, k1, (yo, ssk) to 1 st from m, m1R, k1, sm, k1, m1L, (k2tog, yo) to 3 sts from end, k1, ssk.

Row 12: K to end.

Rows 13-16: Work Rows 11-12 twice.

Row 17: K3, (yo, ssk) to 1 st from m, m1R, k1, sm, k1, m1L, (k2tog, yo) to 3 sts from m, k3, sm, k3, (yo, ssk) to 1 st from m, m1R, k1, sm, k1, m1L, (k2tog, yo) to 3 sts from end, k3. *4 sts increased.*

Row 18: K to end.

Rows 19-24: Work Rows 3-4 3 times.

Rows 25-32: Repeat Rows 9-16. *200 sts.*

Movement 5

Row 1: K to 1 st from m, m1R, k1, sm, k1, m1L, (k2tog, yo) to 3 sts from m, k3, sm, k3, (yo, ssk) to 1 st from m, m1R, k1, sm, k1, m1L, (k2tog, yo) to 3 sts from end, k3.

Row 2 and all foll even-numbered rows: K to end.

Row 3: BO all sts of the first section, up to the first marker. You will have to remove this marker and you will be left with 1 st on your right needle (*the first st of the second section*). M1L, (k2tog, yo) to 2 sts from m, ssk, sm, k2tog, (yo, ssk) to 1 st from m, m1R, k1, sm, k1, m1L, (k2tog, yo) to 2 sts from end, ssk.

Row 5: BO 8 sts, (k2tog, yo) to 2 sts from m, ssk, sm, k2tog, (yo, ssk) to 1 st from m, m1R, k1, sm, k1, m1L, (k2tog, yo) to 2 sts from end, ssk.

Row 7: BO 9 sts, (k2tog, yo) to 2 sts from m, ssk, sm, k2tog, (yo, ssk) to 1 st from m, m1R, k1, sm, k1, m1L, (k2tog, yo) to 2 sts from end, ssk.

Row 9: BO 9 sts, (k2tog, yo) to 2 sts from m, k2, sm, k2, (yo, ssk) to 1 st from m, m1R, k1, sm, k1, m1L, (k2tog, yo) to 2 sts from end, k2.

Row 11: BO 9 sts, (k2tog, yo) to 3 sts from m, k1, ssk, sm, k2tog , k1, (yo, ssk) to 1 st from m, m1R, k1, sm, k1, m1L, (k2tog, yo) to 3 sts from end, k1, ssk

Row 13: BO all the remaining sts of the second section up to the 2nd marker. You will have to remove the 2nd marker and you will be left with 1 st on your right needle (the first st of the third section). K to 1 st before next marker, m1R, k1, sm, m1L, (k2tog, yo) to 3 sts from end, k1, ssk.

Row 15: BO all the remaining sts of the third section up to the 3rd marker. You will have to remove the 3rd marker and you will be left with 1 st on your right needle (the first st of the fourth section). M1L, (k2tog, yo) to 3 sts from end, k1, ssk

Row 17: BO4, (k2tog, yo) to 3 sts from end, k3.

Row 19: BO 5, (k2tog, yo) to 2 sts from end, ssk.

Rows 21 and 23: Same as row 19.

Row 25: BO 5, (k2tog, yo) to 2 sts from end, k2.

Row 27: BO 5, (k2tog, yo) to 3 sts from end, k1, ssk.

Rows 29 and 31: Same as row 27.

Row 33: BO all remaining sts.

Finishing

Weave in ends and block shawl to measurements.

anemone

by veera välimäki

Coral power to the max! This lovely summer top is wonderful to wear and fun to knit. The simple asymmetric shape is made with short rows, nicely minimizing the need for purl stitches. Speckles make this color even more perfect!

anemone

Sizes

XS (S, M, L, XL, 2XL). Shown in size S on a 36½" bust.

Finished chest circumference: 34 (38, 42, 46, 50, 54)" [85 (95, 105, 115, 125, 135) cm]. Choose a size with approx. 2 to 4" [5-10 cm] of positive ease.

Materials

Yarn: 3 (3, 3, 3, 4, 4) skeins of Skinny Singles by Hedgehog Fibres (100% Merino Wool; 400 yds [366 m] / 100 g). Approx. 840 (900, 1000, 1100, 1240, 1360) yds [770 (830, 920, 1000, 1130, 1250) m] of fingering weight yarn. The sample was knit in *Interpretations* special colorway Anemone.

Needles: US 6 [4 mm] and US 4 [3.5 mm] circular needle, 32" [80 cm] long, and dpns in smaller size. Adjust needle size if necessary to obtain the correct gauge.

Other: Stitch markers, tapestry needle and blocking aids.

Gauge

24 sts and 32 rows = 4" [10 cm] in St st using larger needles.

Finished Measurements

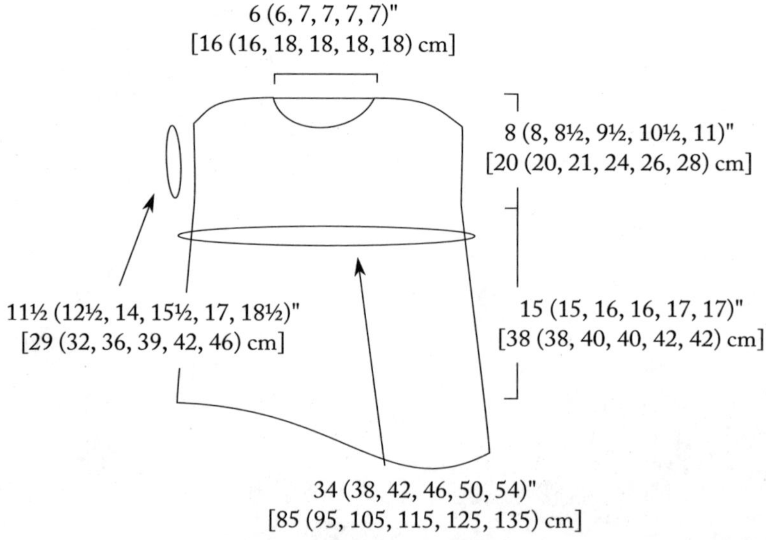

anemone

Upper Back

Using larger circular needle and long-tail cast on, CO 102 (114, 126, 138, 150, 162) sts. Do not join in round. Begin short row shaping as follows:

Row 1 (RS): Knit to last 23 sts, W&T.

Row 2 (WS): Purl to last 23 sts, W&T.

Row 3 (RS): Knit to previous wrapped stitch, k2tog the wrap together with the wrapped st making sure the wrap stays on WS, k1, W&T.

Row 4 (WS): Purl to previous wrapped stitch, ssp the wrap together with the wrapped st making sure the wrap stays on WS, p1, W&T.

Repeat ***Rows 3 and 4*** – 8 more times. Continue even in St st until the piece measures 6 (6½, 7, 8, 8½, 9)" [15 (16, 18, 20, 21, 23) cm] at each end. Cut yarn.

Right Shoulder

Using the same larger needle and with RS of the piece facing, pick up and knit 33 (39, 42, 48, 54, 60) sts from the right shoulder, starting from the sleeve end. *Note: the pick-up row is your next RS row, Row 5; you will then continue with short rows on WS.*

Row 6 (WS, begin short row shaping): Purl to last 23 sts, W&T.

Row 7 (RS): Knit to end.

Row 8 (WS): Purl to previous wrapped stitch, ssp the wrap together with the wrapped st making sure the wrap stays on WS, p1, W&T.

Row 9 (RS): Knit to end.

Repeat ***Short Rows 8 and 9*** – 8 more times. Then continue working whole rows in St st and pick up the last remaining wrap when you come to it. Work in St st until the neck edge measures 4 (4, 4½, 4½, 5, 5)" [10 (10, 12, 12, 13, 13) cm]. Begin neck increases on next RS row.

Increase row (RS): Knit to last 4 sts, m1R, k4.

Repeat the ***Increase Row*** – five more times on every RS row. *You should have 39 (45, 48, 54, 60, 66) sts on needle; 6 sts increased.* End with the last increase row (RS). Cut yarn and leave sts on needle.

left Shoulder

Using the same larger needle and with RS of the back piece facing, pick up and knit 33 (39, 42, 48, 54, 60) sts from the left shoulder, starting from the neck end. *Note: the pick-up row is your next RS row; you will then continue with one whole row on WS.*

Row 10 (WS): Purl to end.

Row 11 (RS, begin short row shaping): Knit to last 23 sts, W&T.

Row 12 (WS): Purl to end.

Row 13 (RS): Knit to previous wrapped stitch, k2tog the wrap together with the wrapped st making sure the wrap stays on WS, k1, W&T.

Row 14 (WS): Purl to end.

Repeat ***Short Rows 13 and 14*** – 8 more times. Then continue working whole rows in St st and pick up the last remaining wrap when you come to it. Work in St st until the neck edge measures 4 (4, 4½, 4½, 5, 5)" [10 (10, 12, 12, 13, 13) cm]. Begin neck increases on next RS row.

Increase row (RS): K4, m1L, knit to end.

Repeat the ***Increase Row*** – five more times on every RS row. *You should have 39 (45, 48, 54, 60, 66) sts on needle; 6 sts increased.* End with the last increase row (RS). Keep yarn attached.

Front

Join shoulders on next WS row as follows: Purl to end of left shoulder stitches, CO 24 (24, 30, 30, 30, 30) sts using backwards-loop CO, purl to end of right shoulder sts. *You should have 102 (114, 126, 138, 150, 162) sts on needle.*

Continue working back and forth in St st until the piece measures 6 (6½, 7, 8, 8½, 9)" [15 (16, 18, 20, 21, 23) cm] at each end. End with a WS row.

Join Back and Fronts

Joining round (RS): PM for BOR, knit the front sts, pm for side, knit the back stiches.

You should have 204 (228, 252, 276, 300, 324) sts on needles.

Body

Work 4" [10 cm] in St st and slip the side seam stitches, the first stitch after each marker, on every second round, ending with a slipped stitches round. Work increases and begin short row shaping on following round:

Short row 15 (RS, increases): Sm, knit to 18 sts before next marker, pm, *k1fb, k1fbf; repeat from * to marker, sm, *k1fbf, k1fb; repeat from * 8 more times, pm, W&T. *54 sts increased; you should have 258 (282, 306, 330, 354, 378) sts on needles.*

Short row 16 (WS): Sm, purl to marker, sm, purl to marker, sm, W&T.

Short row 17 (RS): Sm, knit to m, sm, k10, W&T.

Short row 18 (WS): Purl to m, remove marker (side marker), purl 10, W&T.

Short row 19 (RS): Knit to previous wrapped stitch, k2tog the wrap and the wrapped st, m1L, k2, W&T.

Short row 20 (WS): Purl to previous wrapped stitch, p2tog the wrap and the wrapped st, m1R (purl), p2, W&T.

Repeat ***Rounds 19 and 20*** – 9 more times.

Knit to end and pick up the wrap you come across. Continue in round in St st and begin slanting shaping as follows. *Note: Pick up the last remaining wrap on first round.*

Round 21 (RS): Sm, sl1, knit to 2 sts before m, k2tog, sm, k1, m1L, knit to 1 stitch before marker, m1R, k1, sm, ssk, knit to end.

Round 22 (RS): Sm, knit to end slipping all markers.

Repeat ***Rounds 21 and 22*** until the body measures 13½ (13½, 14½, 14½, 15½, 15½)" [35 (35, 37, 37, 39, 39) cm] from the underarm.

Change to smaller circular needle and work 1½" [3 cm] in garter stitch ribbing (*Round 1: knit all sts; Round 2: *k1, p1; to end of round*). Knit the last round and BO all body stitches.

Finishing

Work the neck line finishing.

Using smaller circular needles pick up and knit 36 (36, 42, 42, 42, 42) sts from the cast-on edge of the back of the neck, pick up and knit 36 (36, 42, 42, 48, 48) sts down the vertical edge of the neck, pick up and knit 24 (24, 30, 30, 30, 30) sts from the cast-on edge of the front and pick up and knit 36 (36, 42, 42, 48, 48) sts up to the shoulder edge.

You should have 132 (132, 156, 156, 168, 168) sts on needles.

Place a BOR marker and knit two rounds. K1b the next round. Knit one more round normally, then BO all neck stitches.

Work the sleeve finishings.

Using smaller dpns and starting from the underarm, pick up and knit 36 (39, 42, 47, 51, 56) sts up to shoulder along the sleeve opening and pick up and knit 36 (39, 42, 47, 51, 56) sts down to underarm.

You should have 72 (78, 84, 94, 102, 112) sts on needles.

Place a BOR marker and knit four rounds. BO sts on next round.

Weave in all yarn ends and block the top to measurements using your preferred method.

explove

Can you picture yourself in a foreign land, a new hemisphere, a location different than your own? Are you eccentric enough to visit a strange new territory, a new dimension?

Would you dare to find nourishment in foreign spices, eat meals made on the streets? Would you rub shoulders with the locals just to feel like someone else for a time... unique perfumes and bodies unusually close.

Many new revelations, emotions confused, things seem backwards when you are the minority, a blank canvas in a place with colors never seen before. The influx of senses can be a terrifying delight.

The strangeness of this new land, at times, would overwhelm you, scare you, send chills through your body. If you choose this path, this exploration of awareness, you would be forever changed. Your mindset evolved, things you once thought essential may be no longer.

Now totally lost and confused, will you be brave enough to continue?
To gloriously roll around, exposed, susceptible, in the sheets of a new land.

Feasting on this crusade with excitement, your days are consumed heedlessly. Those moments of exploration and discovery are the richness of life, where memories and stories, for better or for worse, are born.

When you return, I'll still know and love you. You will be, braver, stronger, wiser, different. Try to make time to be brave, make sacrifices and explore, the world isn't as big as it seems yet is more than you will ever be able to swallow. Don't waste a moment.

explore

glacier tunic

chasing light shawl

glacier tunic

by joji locatelli

I've wanted to explore this construction for a long time. In this tunic, back and front start as small triangles and then the rest of the sweater is knit with increases and decreases to create a biased fabric.

It is worked in the round, with no seams, and with raglan sleeves. You can knit this to any length! As a shorter top or as a long dress.

glacier tunic

Sizes

XS (S, M, L, XL, XXL, 3XL, 4XL). Shown in size M on a 36" bust.

Bust circumference: 29 (32, 36, 40, 44, 48, 52, 56)" [72.5 (80, 90, 100, 110, 120, 130, 140) cm]. Recommended ease: 0-2" [0-5 cm] of negative ease. *See Schematics below and more finished measurements at the end of this pattern.*

Materials

Yarn: 4 (4, 5, 5, 5, 6, 6, 7) skeins of Merino Singles by La Bien Aimée (100% Merino; 400 yds [366 m] / 100 g) or approx. 1520 (1600, 1680, 1800, 1880, 2120, 2280, 2520) yds [1390 (1464, 1537, 1647, 1720, 1940, 2085, 2305) m] of fingering weight yarn. The sample was made using *Interpretations* special colorway Glacier.

Needles: US 4 [3.5 mm] and US 2 [2.75 mm] circular needles, at least 32" [80 cm] long.

Other: Stitch markers, stitch holders or waste yarn, tapestry needle.

Gauge

23 sts and 38 rows = 4" [10 cm] in stockinette stitch on US 4 [3.5 mm] needles. *Before you measure, please take the time to wash and block your swatch in the same manner that you will wash and block your sweater.*

Finished Measurements

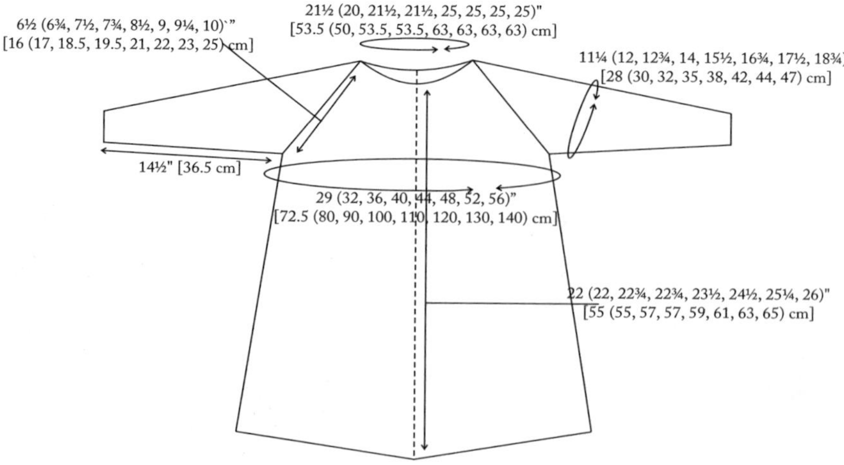

glacier tunic

Back

With US 4 needles [3.5mm], CO 8 sts.

Set-up row: K2, p1, pm, p2, pm, p1, k2.

Row 1 (RS): K2, m1L, k1, m1R, sm, k2, sm, m1L, k1, m1R, k2. *You should have 12 sts.*

Row 2 (WS): K2, p to m, sm, p2, sm, p to 2 sts from end, k2.

Row 3: K2, m1L, k to m, m1R, sm, k2, sm, m1L, k to 2 st from end, m1R, k2. *You should have 16 sts.*

Row 4: K2, p to m, sm, p2, sm, p to 2 sts from end, k2.

Rows 5-6: Same as Rows 3-4. *20 sts*

Row 7: Same as row 3. *24 sts*

Row 8: K to end (Purl ridge).

Repeat ***Rows 3-8*** 2 (2, 2, 2, 3, 3, 3, 3) more times. *You should have 48 (48, 48, 48, 60, 60, 60, 60) sts.*

Break yarn and put all sts on hold.

Front

With US 4 needles [3.5mm], CO 8 sts.

Sizes XS (S, M, L)

Set-up row: K2, p1, pm, p2, pm, p1, k2.

Row 1 (RS): K2, m1L, k1, m1R, sm, k2, sm, m1L, k1, m1R, k2. *You should have 12 sts.*

Row 2 (WS): K2, p to m, sm, p2, sm, p to 2 sts from end, k2.

Row 3: K2, m1L, k to m, m1R, sm, k2, sm, m1L, k to 1 st from end, m1R, k2. *You should have 16 sts.*

Row 4: K2, m1R (purl), p to m, sm, p2, sm, p to 2 sts from end, m1L (purl), k2. *18 sts.*

Rows 5-6: Same as rows 3-4. *24 sts.*

Row 7: Same as row 3. *28 sts.*

Row 8: K2, m1R, k to 2 sts from end, m1L, k2 (Purl ridge). *30 sts.*

Repeat ***Rows 3-8*** once more. *You should have 48 sts.*

Sizes XL (XXL, 3XL, 4XL)

Set-up row: K2, p1, pm, p2, pm, p1, k2.

Row 1 (RS): K2, m1L, k1, m1R, sm, k2, sm, m1L, k1, m1R, k2. *You should have 12 sts.*

Row 2 (WS): K2, p to m, sm, p2, sm, p to 2 sts from end, k2.

Row 3: K2, m1L, k to m, m1R, sm, k2, sm, m1L, k to 1 st from end, m1R, k1. *You should have 16 sts.*

Row 4: K2, m1R (purl), p to m, sm, p2, sm, p to 2 sts from end, m1L (purl), k2. *18 sts.*

Row 5: Same as row 3.

Row 6: K2, m1R, k to 2 sts from end, m1L, k2 (Purl ridge). *24 sts.*

Row 7: Same as row 3.

Row 8: K2, m1R (purl), p to m, sm, p2, sm, p to 2 sts from end, m1L (purl), k2. *30 sts.*

Repeat ***Rows 3-8*** once and then ***Rows 3-6*** once more. *You should have 60 sts.*

Join in the Round

Round 1: K1, m1L, k to m, m1R, sm, k2, sm, m1L, k to 1 st from end, m1R, k1. Pm, CO 18 (14, 18, 18, 18, 18, 18, 18) sts, pm. Place the sts you had on hold for the back on the needles. K1, m1L, k to m, m1R, sm, k2, sm, m1L, k to 1 st from end, m1R, k1. Pm, CO 18 (14, 18, 18, 18, 18, 18, 18) sts. Place beginning of the round marker (*you can use a different style here to differentiate it from the other markers*). Join for working in the round.

You should have 140 (132, 140, 140, 164, 164, 164, 164) sts on the needles.

Round 2: K to end of round.

Round 3: [K to m, m1R, sm, k2, sm, m1L, k to m, sm, m1R, k to m, m1L, sm] twice. *8 sts increased.*

Round 4: K to end of round.

Round 5: [K to m, m1R, sm, k2, sm, m1L,k to m, sm, m1R, k to m, m1L, sm] twice. *8 sts increased.*

Round 6: [K1, p to m, sm, p2, sm, p to 1 st from m, k1, sm, k to m, sm] twice (Purl ridge).

Round 7-8: Same as rounds 3-4. *8 sts increased.*

Repeat ***Rounds 3-8*** 6 (8, 6, 6, 7, 7, 8, 6) more times.

You should have 94 (106, 94, 94, 112, 112, 118, 106) sts for the back and the front and 60 (68, 60, 60, 66, 66, 72, 60) sts for each sleeve.

Yoke Section 2

Sizes XS (S)

Round 1: [K2tog, k to m, m1R, sm, k2, sm, m1L, k to 2 sts from m, ssk, sm, k to m, sm] twice.

Round 2: K to end of round.

Repeat these 2 rounds 2 (5) more times. Your st count doesn't change in this section.

Sizes M (L, XL, XXL, 3XL, 4XL)

Round 1: [K to m, m1R, sm, k2, sm, m1L, k to m, sm, k to m, sm] twice. *4 sts increased.*

Round 2: K to end of round.

Round 3: [K to m, m1R, sm, k2, sm, m1L, k to m, sm, m1R, k to m, m1L, sm] twice. *8 sts increased.*

Round 4: [K1, p to m, sm, p2, sm, p to 1 st from m, k1, sm, k to m, sm] twice (Purl ridge).

Round 5: Same as round 1. *4 sts increased.*

Round 6: K to end of round.

Round 7: Same as round 3. *8 sts increased.*

Round 8: K to end of round.

Round 9: Same as round 1. *4 sts increased.*

Round 10: Same as round 4 (Purl ridge).

Round 11: Same as round 3. *8 sts increased.*

Round 12: K to end of round.

12 sts increased for the body and 6 sts increased for the sleeves.

Size M: Repeat Rounds 1-12 once more.

Sizes L: Repeat Rounds 1-12 once more and then rounds 1-10 once more.

Size XL: Repeat Rounds 1-12 once more.

Size XXL: Repeat Rounds 1-12 twice more.

Size 3XL: Repeat Rounds 1-12 twice more and then rounds 1-4 once more.

Size 4XL: Repeat Rounds 1-12 4 more times and then Rounds 1-2 once more.

All sizes: *You should have 94 (106, 118, 128, 136, 148, 158, 168) sts for the back and the front and 60 (68, 72, 76, 78, 84, 92, 90) sts for each sleeve.*

Divide for body and sleeves

Round 1: K to m, m1R, sm, k2, sm, m1L, k to m, remove m. Place the next 60 (68, 72, 76, 78, 84, 92, 90) sts on hold using a length of waste yarn. CO 1 (1, 2, 2, 5, 6, 7, 9) sts, pm, CO 1 (1, 2, 2, 5, 6, 7, 9) sts, remove m, k to m, m1R, sm, k2, sm, m1L, k to m, remove m. Place the next 60 (68, 72, 76, 78, 84, 92, 90) sts on hold. CO 1 (1, 2, 2, 5, 6, 7, 9) sts, place BOR (beginning of the round) marker, CO 1 (1, 2, 2, 5, 6, 7, 9) sts.

You should have 196 (220, 248, 268, 296, 324, 348, 376) sts.

Round 2: K to end of round.

Round 3: [K2tog, k to m, m1R, sm, k2, sm, m1L, k to 2 sts from m, ssk, sm] twice.

Round 4: K to end of round.

Round 5-6: Repeat Rounds 3-4.

Round 7: [K to m, m1R, sm, k2, sm, m1L, k to m] twice. *No side decreases on this round. 4 sts increased.*

Round 8: K to end of round.

Repeat ***Rounds 3-8*** until work measures 21½ (21½, 22½, 22½, 23¼, 24, 24¾, 25½)" [54 (54, 56, 56, 58, 60, 62, 64) cm from the cast on edge on the front neck, measured along the central spine.

Bottom Shaping

Up to this point, your sweater has a pointy bottom. In these sections you work incomplete rows to give the sweater a straight bottom hem.

Row 1: Break yarn. Slip all sts to the right needle until you reach the first marker, remove m, slip 1 more st, place marker again. Rejoin yarn. Slip next st to right needle, remove marker, place the st back on the left needle. Ssk, k to 2 sts before next marker, ssk, sm, k2tog, k to 1 st before next marker. Slip next st to right needle, remove m, place the st back on the left needle, k2tog. Place marker again. Turn work.

Row 2: P2tog, p to m, sm, p to 2 sts from next marker, p2tog, turn work.

Row 3: You can now remove the marker at the

beginning of this row. Ssk, k to 2 sts from m, ssk, sm, k2tog, k to 2 sts from next m, k2tog, turn work.

Row 4: You can now remove the marker at the beginning of this row. P2tog, p to m, sm, p to 2 sts before last turning point, P2tog, turn work.

Row 5: Ssk, k to m, sm, k to 2 sts from last turning point, k2tog, turn work. (*No 'side' decreases on this row*).

Row 6: P2tog, p to 2 sts from last turning point, P2tog, turn work.

Row 7: Ssk, k to 2 sts before m, ssk, sm, k2tog, k to 2 sts from last turning point, k2tog, turn work.

Row 8: Same as row 6.

Row 9: Same as row 7.

Row 10: Same as row 6.

Repeat ***Rows 5-10*** until you only have 1 st left at each side of the marker. Remove this marker, k2tog, fasten off.

You still have the sts for the other half of the sweater on the needles. Rejoin yarn to start working a RS row over the first of these stitches.

Row 1: Slip first st to right needle, remove marker, place the st back on the left needle. Ssk, k to 2 sts before next marker, ssk, sm, k2tog, k to 2 sts before next marker, k2tog. Turn work.

Row 2: P2tog, p to m, sm, p to 2 sts from end, p2tog.

Row 3: Ssk, k to 2 sts from m, ssk, sm, k2tog, k to 2 sts from end, k2tog.

Row 4: P2tog, p to 2 sts from end, p2tog.

Row 5: Ssk, k to m, sm, k to 2 sts from end, k2tog. (*No 'side' decreases on this row*).

Row 6: P2tog, p to 2 sts from end, p2tog.

Row 7: Ssk, k to 2 sts before m, ssk, sm, k2tog, k to 2 sts from end, k2tog.

Row 8: Same as row 6.

Row 9: Same as row 7.

Row 10: Same as row 6.

Repeat ***Rows 5-10*** until you only have 1 st left at each side of the marker. Remove this marker, k2tog, fasten off.

Neckline

With US 2 [2.75 mm] needles, starting at the right corner of the back neck, pick up and knit approx. 40 (40, 40, 40, 50, 50, 50, 50) sts along the back neck, 16 (12, 16, 16, 16, 16, 16, 16) sts from the top of one sleeve, 46 (46, 46, 46, 56, 56, 56, 56) sts from the front neck, 16 (12, 16, 16, 16, 16, 16, 16) sts from the other sleeve. Place marker and join for working in the round.

Next round: (K1, p1) to end of round.

Work 6 more rounds in the established pattern.

BO all sts loosely in pattern.

Sleeves

Place the sts from one of the sleeves onto the larger needle. Starting at the centre of the armhole, pick up and knit 1 (2, 2, 2, 4, 5, 6, 8) sts, k to end. Pick up 1 (2, 2, 2, 4, 5, 6, 8) more sts, reaching the centre of the armhole again. (The number of sts to pick up from the underarm is not necessarily the same as the sts you CO when joining the body). Pm to indicate beginning of the round. *You should have 62 (72, 76, 80, 86, 94, 104, 106) sts on the needles.*

Work in Stockinette st for 18 rounds.

Next round - Decrease round: K1, ssk, k to 3 sts from m, k2tog, k1.

Continue working in stockinette stitch repeating a decrease round every 20th (12th, 12th,10th, 9th, 7th, 6th, 6th) following round until you have worked a total of 6 (10, 10, 11, 13, 17, 20, 20) decrease rounds. *You should now have 50 (52, 56, 58, 60, 60, 64, 66) sts.*

Then continue working in pattern until sleeve measures 14" [35 cm].

Switch to US 2 [2.75mm] needles.

Next round: (K1, p1) to end of round.

Work 6 more rounds in the established ribbing.

BO all sts loosely in pattern.

Finishing

Sew in ends and block garment to finished measurements.

Finished Measurements

Bust circumference: 29 (32, 36, 40, 44, 48, 52, 56)" [72.5 (80, 90, 100, 110, 120, 130, 140) cm].

Neck opening: 21½ (20, 21½, 21½, 25, 25, 25, 25)" [53.5 (50, 53.5, 53.5, 63, 63, 63, 63) cm].

Length from front neckline to bottom hem: 22 (22, 22¾, 22¾, 23½, 24½, 25¼, 26)" [55 (55, 57, 57, 59, 61, 63, 65) cm].

Yoke depth: 6½ (6¾, 7½, 7¾, 8½, 9, 9¼, 10)" [16 (17, 18.5, 19.5, 21, 22, 23, 25) cm].

Upper arm circumference: 11¼ (12, 12¾, 14, 15½, 16¾, 17½, 18¾)" [28 (30, 32, 35, 38, 42, 44, 47) cm].

Sleeve length: 14½" [36.5 cm].

chasing light

by veera välimäki

A lovely light lace shawl with a lot of garter stitch! Chasing light Shawl is wonderful to work on and even lovelier to wear. This yarn is a true Walk Collection colorway: so rich and deep, yet in the end a perfect light grey!

chasing light

Sizes

One Size

Finished measurements: 82" [208 cm] long and 23" [58 cm] deep at deepest spot.

Materials

Yarn: 2 skeins of Luxe Light by Walk Collection (70% alpaca, 20% silk, 10% cashmere; 656 yds [600 m] / 100 g). Approx. 880 yds [800 m] of heavy lace weight yarn. The sample was knit in *Interpretations* special colorway Out of the Dark.

Needles: US 4 [3.5 mm] circular needle, 32" [80 cm] long. Adjust needle size if necessary to obtain the correct gauge.

Other: Stitch marker, tapestry needle and blocking aids. Optional, but recommended: row counter.

Gauge

18 sts and 34 rows = 4" [10 cm] in garter stitch.

Finished Measurements

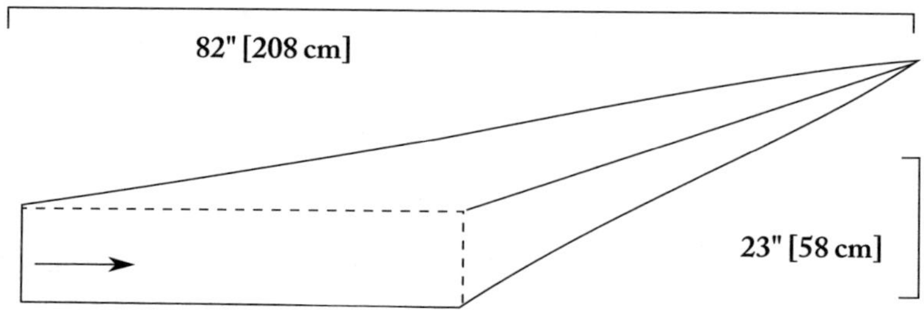

chasing light

lace Part

Using circular needle and long-tail cast on, CO 71 sts. Do not join. Work 10 rows in garter stitch (*knit on RS and WS*). Begin lace as follows:

Row 1 (RS): K5, p1, work row 1 of Chart A three times, k5.

Row 2 (WS): K5, work the next row of Chart A three times, k6.

Row 3 (RS): K5, p1, work the next row of Chart A three times, k5.

Row 4 (WS): K5, work the next row of Chart A three times, k6.

Repeat ***Rows 3 and 4*** – 100 more times, or until the length is two times the width (approx. 31.5" [80 cm]), ending with a WS row.

Garter Stitch Part

Next you will continue in garter stitch and pick up stitches from the long edge of the rectangle as follows.

Row 5 (RS): Knit to end, pm and continue with RS facing pick up 142 sts along the long edge of the rectangle. *You should have 213 sts on needle.*

Row 6 (WS): K1, ssk, knit to m, sm, knit to end.

Row 7 (RS): K1, k2tog, knit to 1 st before marker, m1R, k1, sm, k1, m1L, knit to last 3 sts, ssk, k1.

Row 8 (WS): K1, ssk, knit to m, sm, knit to end.

Row 9 (RS): K1, k2tog, knit to m, sm, k1, m1L, knit to last 3 sts, ssk, k1.

Row 10 (WS): K1, ssk, knit to m, sm, knit to end.

Repeat ***Rows 7 to 10*** - 68 times more. *You should have 5 sts on needle.* BO remaining stitches on following row (RS).

Finishing

Weave in all yarn ends and block the shawl using your preferred method.

Chart A for lace

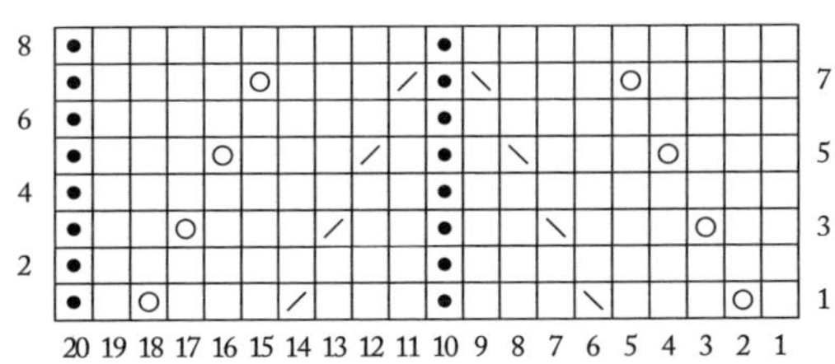

□ St st; knit on RS, purl on WS

⊡ Rev St st; purl on RS, knit on WS

⊙ yo, yarnover

⧅ ssk

⧄ k2tog

rough

I confess to long hours of daydreams sitting at my kitchen table gazing out through the curtains. The hush of dusk brings fond memories of times we shared.

The light passes through curtains of white casting burnt edges to the lace. Shadows of a time long past and days worn through.

Walking through the meadow kicking dandelions all around us. It is so peaceful out there. The sun warming our heads and shoulders like a melting blanket, so hot it sends goosebumps down your arms.

Twisting daisy chains, we'd talk for hours about all the things that make us happy and sad. Dancing with invisible heros we were barefoot primitives in the forest yet princesses in our minds.

Years have made us older and tougher, like leather hides, still soft yet somehow smoother.

Our conversations are still a collection of fabrics stitched together in my mind. Although far from each other now I'll always have those times.

rough

reflection shawl

rugged coat

rugged coat

by joji locatelli

Perfect yet rough, unfinished, this is a modern square style coat, with very little shaping. It is worked from the top down using a textured stitch and simple cables down the front and the back.

rugged coat

Sizes

XS/S (M/L, XL/XXL, 3XL/4XL). Shown in size M on a 36" bust.

To fit bust size 28-35 (36-42, 44-52, 54-62)" [70-87.5 (90-105, 110-130, 135-155) cm]. Recommended ease: 5-10" of positive ease (shown with 10" of positive ease). *See Schematics below.*

Materials

Yarn: 7 (8, 10, 12) skeins of Tosh DK by Madelinetosh (100% Merino; 225 yds [206 m] / skein) or approx. 1575 (1800, 2250, 2700) yds [1440 (1650, 2060, 2475) m] of DK weight yarn. The sample was made using *Intepretations* special colorway Pebble.
Needles: US 6 [4 mm] circular needles, at least 32" [80 cm] long.

Other: Stitch markers, cable needle, stitch holders or waste yarn, tapestry needle.

Gauge

20 sts and 30 rows = 4" [10 cm] in Broken Rib on US 6 [4 mm] needles. *Before you measure, please take the time to wash and block your swatch in the same manner that you will wash and block your sweater.*

Finished Measurements

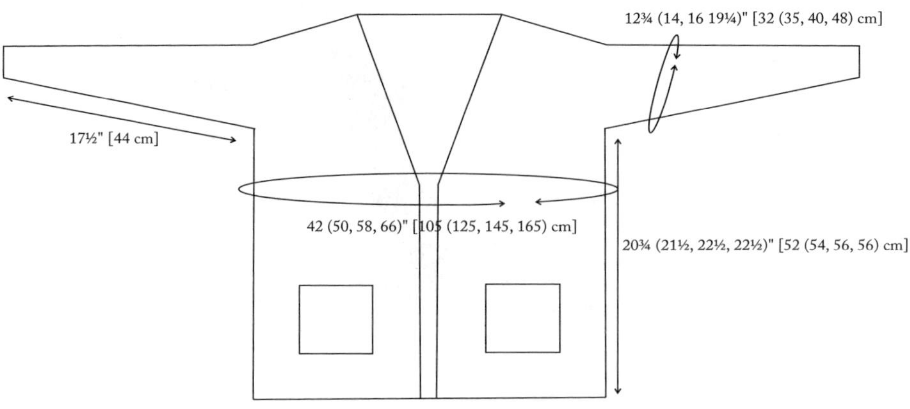

rugged coat

Stitches Used

Broken Rib (worked over an odd number of sts)

Row 1 (RS): Knit all sts.

Row 2: P1, (k1, p1) to end.

Repeat ***Rows 1-2*** for pattern.

Cable (worked over 16 sts)

Row 1: C8B (slip 4 onto cable needle and hold in back, k4, k4 from CN), C8F (slip 4 onto CN and hold in front, k4, k4 from CN).

Rows 2, 4, 6, 8, 10, 12: Purl 16.

Rows 3, 5, 7, 9, 11: Knit 16.

Repeat ***Rows 1-12*** for pattern.

Directions

Right Collar

In this section, slip all sts pwise unless otherwise noted.

CO 8 sts using a long tail cast on.

Row 1 (RS): Sl1, k to end.

Row 2 (WS): Sl1, k1, (p1, k1) to end.

Repeat ***Rows 1-2*** until work measures 2¾ (3¼, 3½, 3½)" [7 (8, 9, 9) cm] from your CO edge.

Right Shoulder

Row 1 (RS): With the knitted CO method, CO 42 (50, 58, 68) sts. K17 (23, 29, 35), pm, k16, pm, k to end of row. *You should have 50 (58, 66, 76) sts on the needles.*

Row 2(WS): Sl1, (k1, p1) 4 (5, 6, 8) times, W&T.

Row 3: K to end.

Row 4: Sl1, (k1, p1) to last wrapped st, (k1, p1) 3 times -no need to pick up the wrap if it's not indicated-, W&T.

Row 5: K to end.

Row 6: Sl1, (k1, p1) to last wrapped st, k1, p1, sm, p4, W&T.

Row 7 and all following RS rows: K to end (slipping markers).

Row 8: Sl1, (k1, p1) to m, sm, p to last wrapped st and purl it tog with wrap, p6, W&T.

Row 10: Sl1, (k1, p1) to m, sm, p to last wrapped st and purl it tog with wrap, p to m, sm, p1, W&T.

Row 12: Sl1, (k1, p1) to m, sm, p to m, sm, p1, (k1, p1) 4 times, W&T.

Row 14: Sl1, (k1, p1) to m, sm, p to m, sm, p1, (k1, p1) to last wrapped st, (k1, p1) 4 times , W&T.

Sizes XS/S (M/L)

Row 15: K to end (slipping markers).

Row 16: Sl1, (k1, p1) to m, sm, p to m, sm, p1, (k1, p1) to end of row.

Sizes XL/XXL (3XL/4XL)

Row 15: K to end (slipping markers).

Row 16: Sl1, (k1, p1) to m, sm, p to m, sm, p1, (k1, p1) to last wrapped st, (k1, p1) 4 times , W&T.

Row 17: K to end (slipping markers).

Row 18: Sl1, (k1, p1) to m, sm, p to m, sm, p1, (k1, p1) to end of row.

Right Front

Set-up row 1 (RS): Sl1, k to m, sm, work row 1 of CABLE, sm, k to 6 sts from end, pm, k to end.

Set-up row 2 (WS): Sl1, k1, (p1, k1) to m, sm, p1, (k1, p1) to m, sm, work foll row of Cable, sm, p1, (k1, p1) to end.

Row 1: Sl1, k to m, sm, work foll row of Cable, sm, k to next m, m1L, sm, k to end.

Rows 2, 4, 6: Sl1, k1, (p1, k1) to m, sm, (k1, p1) to m, sm, work foll row of Cable, sm, p1, (k1, p1) to end.

Row 3, 5: Sl1, k to m, sm, work foll row of Cable, sm, k to end.

Row 7: Sl1, k to m, sm, work foll row of Cable, sm, k to next m, m1L, sm, k to end.

Row 8, 10, 12: Sl1, k1, (p1, k1) to m, sm, p1,

(k1, p1) to m, sm, work foll row of Cable, sm, p1, (k1, p1) to end.

Row 9, 11: Sl1, k to m, sm, work foll row of Cable, sm, k to end.

Repeat ***Rows 1-12*** until work measures 6½ (7, 8, 9½)" [16 (17.5, 20, 24) cm] from CO edge (measured along the sleeve edge), ending with a WS row. Break yarn and put on all sts on hold. Take note of the row of the Cable repeat that you end on so you can make the other pieces to match.

Note: You will continue to work more neck increases after joining the body.

left Collar

With the RS facing you, pick up and knit 8 sts from the CO edge of the right collar.

Row 1 (WS): Sl1, p1 (k1, p1) to end.

Row 2 (RS): Sl1, k to end.

Repeat ***Rows 1-2*** until work measures 2¾ (3¼, 3½, 3½)" [7 (8, 9, 9) cm] from the pick up edge, ending with a WS row.

left Shoulder

Row 1 (RS): Sl1, k to end of row. With knitted CO method, CO 42 (50, 58, 68) sts. *You should have 50 (58, 66, 76) sts on the needles.*

Row 2 (WS): P1, (k1, p1) 8 (11, 14, 17) times, pm, p16, pm, p1, (k1, p1) to end of row.

Row 3: Sl1, k8 (10, 12, 16), W&T.

Row 4: P1, (k1, p1) to end of row.

Row 5: Sl1, k to last wrapped st, knit it -no need to pick up the wrap unless indicated-, k5, W&T.

Row 6: Same as 4.

Row 7: Sl1, k to marker, sm, k4, W&T.

Row 8: P to m, sm, p1, (k1, p1) to end.

Row 9: Sl1, k to m, sm, k to last wrapped st and knit it tog with wrap, k6, W&T.

Row 10: Same as 8.

Row 11: Sl1, k to m, sm, k to last wrapped st and knit it tog with wrap, k to m, sm, k1, W&T.

Row 12: P1, sm, p to m, sm, p1, (k1, p1) to end.

Row 13: Sl1, k to last wrapped st (slipping markers), k8, W&T.

Row 14: (K1, p1) to m, sm, p to m, sm, p1, (k1, p1) to end.

<u>Sizes XS/S (M/L)</u>

Row 15: Sl1, k to last wrapped st (slipping markers), k to end.

Row 16: Sl1, (p1, k1) to m, sm, p to m, sm, p1, (k1, p1) to end.

<u>Sizes XL/XXL (3XL/4XL)</u>

Row 15: Sl1, k to last wrapped st (slipping markers), k8, W&T.

Row 16: Sl1, k1, (p1, k1) to m, sm, p to m, sm, p1, (k1, p1) to end.

Row 17: Sl1, k k to end slipping markers.

Row 18: Sl1, k1, (p1, k1) to m, sm, p to m, sm, p1, (k1, p1) to end.

left Front

Set-up row 1: Sl1, k5, pm, k to m, sm, work row 1 of CABLE, sm, k to end.

Set-up row 2: Sl1, (k1, p1) to m, sm, work foll row of Cable, sm, p1, (k1, p1) to m, sm, (k1, p1) to end.

Row 1: Sl1, k to m, sm, m1R, k to m, sm, work foll of Cable, sm, k to end.

Rows 2, 4, 6: Sl1, (k1, p1) to m, sm, work foll row of Cable, sm, (p1, k1) to m, sm, (k1, p1) to end.

Rows 3, 5: Sl1, k to m, sm, k to m, sm, work foll row of Cable, sm, k to end.

Row 7: Sl1, k to m, sm, m1R, k to m, sm, work foll of Cable, sm, k to end.

Rows 8, 10, 12: Sl1, (k1, p1) to m, sm, work foll row of Cable, sm, p1, (k1, p1) to m, sm, (k1, p1) to end.

Rows 9, 11: Sl1, k to m, sm, k to m, sm, work foll row of Cable, sm, k to end.

Repeat ***Rows 1-12*** until work measures 6½ (7, 8, 9½)" [16 (17.5, 20, 24) cm] from CO edge (measured along the sleeve edge), ending with the same WS row as you did for the other front. You will later have to resume the knitting over these stitches. If it's possible, put all sts on hold leaving the yarn attached (do not break yarn).

Note: You will continue to work more neck increases after joining the body.

Back

With a different ball of yarn, starting at the sleeve edge of the left shoulder and with RS facing you, pick up and knit 42 (50, 58, 68) sts from the left shoulder CO. Pick up and knit 29 (33, 37, 37) sts from the collar and 42 (50, 58, 68) sts from the right shoulder. *You should have a total of 113 (133, 153, 173) sts on the needles.*

Row 2 (WS): P1, (k1, p1) 8 (11, 14, 17) times, pm, p16, pm, p1, (k1, p1) 19 (23, 27, 31) times, W&T.

Row 3 (RS): K31 (39, 47, 55), W&T.

Row 4: P1, (k1, p1) to last wrapped st, (k1, p1) 3 times, W&T.

Row 5: K to last wrapped st, knit it, k5, W&T.

Row 6: P1, (k1, p1) to last wrapped st, k1, p1, pm, p4, W&T.

Row 7: K to last wrapped st (slipping marker), k2, sm, k4, W&T.

Row 8: P to m, sm, p1, (k1, p1) to m, sm, p to last wrapped st and purl it tog with wrap, p6,W&T.

Row 9: K to last wrapped st (slipping markers), knit it together with wrap, k6, W&T.

Row 10: P to m, sm, p1, (k1, p1) to m, sm, p to last wrapped st and purl it tog with wrap, p4, pm, p1, W&T.

Row 11: K to last wrapped st (slipping markers) and knit it tog with wrap, k to m, sm, k1, W&T.

Row 12: P1, sm, p to m, sm, p1, (k1, p1) to m, sm, p to m, sm, p1, (k1, p1) 4 times, W&T.

Row 13: K to last wrapped st (slipping markers), k8, W&T.

Row 14: P1, (k1, p1) to m, sm, p to m, sm, p1, (k1, p1) to m, sm, p to m, sm, p1, (k1, p1) to end.

<u>Sizes XS/S (M/L)</u>

Row 15: K to last wrapped st (slipping markers), k to end.

Row 16: Sl 1, (k1, p1) to m, sm, p to m, sm, p1, (k1, p1) to m, sm, p to m, sm, p1, (k1, p1) to end.

<u>Sizes XL/XXL (3XL/4XL)</u>

Row 15: K to last wrapped st (slipping markers), k8 W&T.

Row 16: Sl 1, (k1, p1) to m, sm, p to m, sm, p1, (k1, p1) to m, sm, p to m, sm, p1, (k1, p1) 4 times, W&T.

<u>All sizes</u>

Row 17: Sl 1, k to m, sm, work row 1 of CABLE, sm, k to m, sm, work row 1 of CABLE, sm, k to end.

Row 18: Sl1, (k1, p1) to m, sm, work foll row of CABLE, sm, p1, (k1, p1) to m, sm, work foll row of CABLE, sm, p1, (k1, p1) to end.

Row 19: Sl1, k to m, sm, work foll row of CABLE, sm, k to m, sm, work foll row of CABLE, sm, k to end.

Continue working in pattern until work measures 6½ (7, 8, 9½)" [16 (17.5, 20, 24) cm] from the point where you picked up your sts, measured along the sleeve edge, ending on the same WS row as you did for the other pieces. Break yarn and put all sts on hold.

Join Body

Place the sts for the left front that you had on hold back onto the needles. You still had a ball of working yarn attached to them, so get ready to start a RS row.

Row 1: Work in patt to end of row (make a neck increase if necessary in this row). Place the sts you had on hold for the back on the needles, place marker. Work in patt to end of row, place marker. Place the sts you had on hold for the right front on the needle, work in patt to end of row (working a neck increase if necessary).

Row 2: Sl1, work in patt to cable m, sm, work CABLE, sm, p1, (k1, p1) to m, sm, p1, (k1, p1) to m, sm, work CABLE, sm, p1, (k1, p1) to m, sm, work CABLE, sm, p1 (k1, p1) to m, sm, p1, (k1, p1) to m, sm, work CABLE, sm, work in patt to end.

Continue working in pattern and increasing at neck edge as directed before until you have made a total of 12 (14, 16, 16) increases each side. *You should have a total of 237 (277, 317, 361) sts: 62 (72, 82, 94) for each front and 113 (133, 153, 173) for the back.*

Continue working in pattern until work measures 10 (11, 11, 12)" [25 (27.5, 27.5, 30) cm] from the armhole. *Note: I recommend that you end up on rows 6 or 8 of the Cable repeat so that the cables in the pockets start on row 3 or 5. This will make them look better.*

Pockets

Row 1 (RS): Sl1, k22 (24, 26, 28). Place the next 30 sts on hold, pm. CO 25 new sts using the cable CO (see Glossary), pm. Work in patt to 53 (55, 57, 59) sts from end. Place the next 30 sts on hold. Pm, CO 25 new sts, pm, k to end.

Row 2 (WS): Sl1, (k1, p1) to m, sm, k1, (p1, k1) to m, sm, p1, (k1, p1) to m, sm, p1, (k1, p1) to m, sm, work CABLE, sm, p1, (k1, p1) to m, sm, work CABLE, sm, p1, (k1, p1) to m, sm, p1, (k1, p1) to m, sm, k1, (p1, k1) to m, sm, p1, (k1, p1) to end.

Row 3 (RS): Sl1, k to m, sm, k to m, sm, k to m, sm, k to m, sm, work CABLE, sm, k to m, sm, work CABLE, sm, k to m, sm, k to m, sm, k to m, sm, k to end.

Repeat ***Rows 2-3*** twice more and then row 2 once more.

Row 9 (RS): Sl1, k to pocket stitch marker, remove m, k6 (8, 10, 12), pm, (k2, m1L) 5 times, k1, pm, k to m, remove m. Work in pattern to next pocket marker, remove marker. K8 (6, 4, 2), pm, (k2, m1L) 5 times, k1, pm, k to m, remove m, k to end.

Row 10: Sl1, (k1, p1) to m, sm, work CABLE (work the same row you need to work for the back), sm, p1, (k1, p1) to m, [sm, p1, (k1, p1) to m, sm, work CABLE] twice, sm, p1, (k1, p1) to m, sm, p1, (k1, p1) to m, sm, work CABLE, sm, p1, (k1, p1) to end.

Continue working in pattern until work measures 20¾ (21½, 22½, 22½)" [52 (54, 56, 56) cm] from the armhole.

Bind off all sts using a Tubular Bind Off (see Glossary) or any other BO method you prefer.

Pocket linings

Place the sts you had on hold for one of the pocket linings and re-join yarn to begin a RS row.

Work in Stockinette st for 5¼" [13 cm] and then BO all sts. Break yarn.

Repeat for the other pocket lining.

Sleeves

Starting at the bottom centre of the underarm, pick up and knit 63 (69, 79, 95) sts around the armhole. Place marker and join for working in the round.

Round 1: K1, (p1, k1) to end.

Round 2: K to end.

Work in the established pattern for 4" [10 cm].

Next round - Decrease round: K1, p2tog, work in patt to 3 sts from end, p2tog, k1.

Continue working in pattern, but always keeping 1 st at each side of the marker as a Knit stitch.

Repeat the ***Decrease round*** every 20th (12th, 8th, 6th) following round until you have worked a total of 4 (6, 10, 15) decrease rounds. *You should have 55 (57, 59, 65) sts left.*

When sleeve measures 17½" [44 cm] from the armhole (or your desired length), BO all sts using a Tubular Bind Off (see Glossary) or any other BO method you prefer.

Finishing

Weave in all ends and block sweater to measurements. Sew pocket linings to the back of the pockets.

Finished Measurements

Body circumference: 42 (50, 58, 66)" [105 (125, 145, 165) cm].

Length from underarm to bottom hem: 21¼ (21½, 22½, 22½)" [52 (54, 56, 56) cm].

Upper sleeve circumference: 12¾ (14, 16 19¼)" [32 (35, 40, 48) cm].

Sleeve length from underarm to cuff: 17½" [44 cm].

reflection

by veera välimäki

Rough edges and mirroring stitch patterns alternate in this little shawl.
Even if the look is rugged the feel is oh-so soft because of the loveliest of merino.
The colorway is the most magnificent gray with tiniest hints of speckles!

reflection

Sizes

One Size

Finished measurements: 79” [200 cm] long and 18” [45 cm] deep.

Materials

Yarn: 2 skeins of Everyday Sport by The Uncommon Thread (100% Superwash Merino Wool; 330 yds [300 m] / 100 g). Approx. 620 yds [580 m] of sport to light DK weight yarn. The sample was knit in *Interpretations* special colorway Spektor.

Needles: US 7 [4.5 mm] circular needle, 32” [80 cm] long. Adjust needle size if necessary to obtain the correct gauge.

Other: Tapestry needle and blocking aids.

Gauge

16 sts and 32 rows = 4” [10 cm] in garter stitch.

Finished Measurements

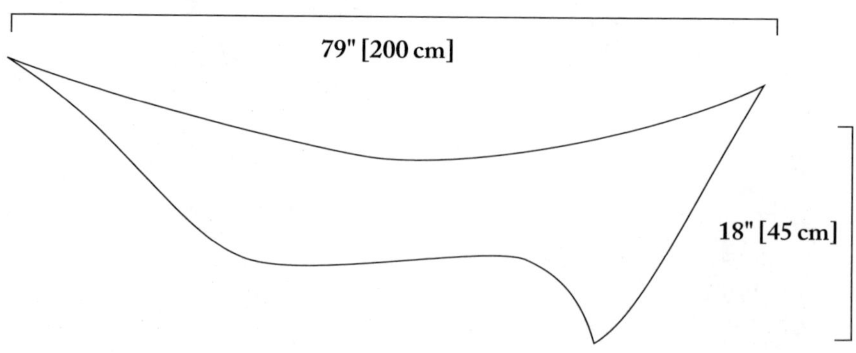

reflection

Garter Stitch Beginning

Using circular needle and long-tail cast on, CO 3 sts.

Row 1 (RS): K1, k1fb, k1.

Row 2 (WS): K1fb, knit to end.

Row 3 (RS): Knit to last 2 stitches, k1fb, k1.

Row 4 (WS): K1fb, knit to end.

Row 5 (RS): K1, k2tog, knit to last 2 stitches, k1fb, k1.

Row 6 (WS): K1fb, knit to end.

Repeat ***Rows 3 to 6*** - 27 more times. *You should have 89 sts on needle.*

First Ribbing

Row 7 (RS): K1fb to last st, k1. *You should have 177 sts on needle.*

Row 8 (WS): K1fb, [k1, p1] to end.

Row 9 (RS): Slip the first stitch, p1, [k1, p1] to last 2 stitches, k1fb, k1.

Row 10 (WS): K1fb, [k1, p1] to end.

Repeat ***Rows 9 and 10*** – 18 more times. *You should have 216 sts on needle.*

First Short Rows

Row 11 (RS): Knit to last 2 stitches, k1fb, k1.

Row 12 (WS): K1fb, knit to end.

Row 13 (RS): K1, k2tog, k4, W&T.

Row 14 (WS): Knit to end.

Row 15 (RS): K1, k2tog, knit to 5 sts after the last wrapped st, W&T.

Row 16 (WS): Knit to end.

Repeat ***Rows 15 and 16*** – 14 more times. *You should have 202 sts on needle.*

Garter Stitch

Row 17 (RS): K1, k2tog, knit to last 2 stitches, k1fb, k1.

Row 18 (WS): K1fb, knit to end.

Work ***Rows 17 and 18*** – 22 more times. *You should have 225 sts on needle.*

Second Ribbing

Row 19 (RS): [K1, p1] to last 3 sts, k1, p1fb, k1.

Row 20 (WS): K1fb, p1, [k1, p1] to end.

Repeat ***Rows 19 and 20*** twice more. *You should have 231 sts on needle.*

Second Short Rows

Row 21 (RS): Knit to last 2 stitches, k1fb, k1.

Row 22 (WS): K1fb, knit to end.

Row 23 (RS): K1, k2tog, k4, W&T.

Row 24 (WS): Knit to end.

Row 25 (RS): K1, k2tog, knit to 5 sts after the last wrapped st, W&T.

Row 26 (WS): Knit to end.

Repeat ***Rows 25 and 26*** – 16 more times. *You should have 215 sts on needle.*

Third Ribbing

Row 27 (RS): [K1 tbl, p1 tbl] to last 3 sts, k1 tbl, p1fb, k1.

Row 28 (WS): K1fb, p1 tbl, [k1 tbl, p1 tbl] to end.

Repeat ***Rows 27 and 28*** twice more. *You should have 221 sts on needle.*

Final ribbing

Row 29 (RS): [K1fb, p1fb] to last st, k1. *You should have 441 sts on needle.*

Row 30 (WS): K1fb, [k2, p2] to end.

Row 31 (RS): [K2, p2] to last 2 sts, k1fb, k1.

Row 32 (WS): K1fb, p2, [k2, p2] to end.

Row 33 (RS): [K2, p2] to last 4 sts, k2, p1fb, k1.

Row 34 (WS): K1fb, [k2, p2] to end.

Repeat ***Rows 31 to 34*** – 15 more times.or until you almost run out of yarn. *You should have 506 sts on needle.* or until you almost run out of yarn. BO all sts in pattern on following RS row.

Finishing

Weave in all yarn ends and block the shawl using your preferred method.

glossary

glossary of terms and useful links

Cable Cast On

www.purlsoho.com/create/cable-cast-on

Kitchener Stitch (or grafting)

www.knitty.com/ISSUEsummer04/FEATtheresasum04

Long-tail CO

www.purlsoho.com/create/2006/09/29/long-tail-cast-on

Tubular Bind Off

www.purlsoho.com/create/long-tail-tubular-bind-off

Provisional cast on

There is a great tutorial by Lucy Neatby on Youtube.
www.youtube.com/watch?v=R3J-sUx_whE

Wrap and Turn

A great tutorial by The Purl Bee on short rows can be found here:
www.purlbee.com/2008/06/18/short-rows

Left Twist (LT)

Insert your needle into the second stitch on your main needle through the back loop and knit the stitch, leaving it on the needle. Bring your working needle around the front of your work and insert your needle into the first stitch knitwise and knit the stitch as normal. Slip both stitches off the main needle together.

abbreviations

approx: Approximately
BO: Bind Off
BOR: Beginning of round
C4B: Slip 2 onto cable needle and hold in back, k2, k2 from CN
C4F: Slip 2 onto cable needle and hold in front, k2, k2 from CN
C6B: Slip 3 onto cable needle and hold in back, k3, k3 from CN
C6F: Slip 3 onto cable needle and hold in front, k3, k3 from CN
C8B: Slip 4 onto cable needle and hold in back, k4, k4 from CN
C8F: Slip 4 onto cable needle and hold in front, k4, k4 from CN
CC: Contrasting Color
CO: Cast On
dpns: Double-pointed needles
foll(s): Follows, following
Garter st: Garter stitch; Back and forth: knit on RS and WS; In the round: knit one round; purl one round
k: Knit
ktbl: Knit through back loop
k1b: Knit one below
k1fb: Knit into front of the stitch, leave stitch on left needle and knit into back of the same stitch; increase
k1fbf: Knit one leaving the stitch on left needle, knit into the back of the same stitch and once more into the front of the stitch (2 sts increased)
k2tog: Knit 2 sts together; decrease
k3tog: Knit 3 sts together; 2 sts decrease
LR: Lace Repeat
LT: Left Twist (see Glossary)
m: marker
MC: Main Color
m1p: Purled increase. With left needle tip, lift strand between needles, from back to front. Purl lifted loop
m1L (purl): Left slanting increase, make one left; pick up the strand between the stitches from front, purl through the back of the stitch
m1R (purl): Right slanting increase, make one right; pick up the strand between the stitches from back, purl through the front of the stitch
m1L: Increase slanted to the left (pick up the horizontal bar btw the sts from front to back, knit through back leg)
m1R: Increase slanted to the right (pick up the horizontal bar btw the sts from back to front, knit through front leg)
patt: Pattern
pm: Place marker
p: Purl
ptbl: Purl through back loop
p1fb: Purl into front of the stitch, leave stitch on left needle and purl into back of the same stitch; increase
p2tog: Purl 2 sts together; decrease
RS: Right side
rev St st: Reverse Stockinette stitch; knit on WS, purl on RS
S2kp: Slip 2 as if to k2tog, pass slipped sts over.
sl: Slip
sm: Slip marker.
ssk: Slip, slip, knit slipped sts tbl; decrease
sssk: Slip, slip, slip, knit slipped sts tbl; 2 sts decrease
ssp: Slip, slip, purl slipped sts tbl; decrease.
st(s): Stitch (stitches)
St st: Stockinette stitch; knit on RS, purl on WS
tbl: Through back loop
tog: Together
twisted rib: In the round: k1tbl, p1, repeat to end of round
WS: Wrong side
W&T: Wrap and turn; work to place stated in pattern, bring yarn front, slip the next st without knitting it, bring the yarn back, slide the slipped st back on left needle, and turn work
yo: Yarn over

special colorways

Fino by Julie Asselin
75% Merino, 15% Cashmere, 10% Silk; 400 yds [366 m] / 115 g. Special colorway Happy.

Titus 4ply by Eden Cottage Yarns
75% Superwash Merino Wool, 25% Silk; 436 yds [400 m] / 100 g. Special colorway Bliss.

Studio Sock by Neighborhood Fiber Co
100% Merino; 400 yds [366 m] / 114 g. Special colorways Navy, Brown Pink, Dark Gray and Denim.

Väinämöinen DK by Louhittaren Luola
75% Superwash Wool, 25% Nylon; 206 yds [185 m] / 100 g. Special colorway Indigo.

Bello Worsted by The Plucky Knitter
55% Merino, 45% Cashmere; 200 yds [183 m] / 105 g. Special colorway Pewter.

House DK by House of A La Mode
100% Merino Wool; 250 yds [195 m] / 115 g. Special colorway Kissed Quartz.

Top Draw Sock by Skein
85% Merino, 15% Nylon; 437 yds [400 m] / 95 g. Special colorways Sway (pale blue), Flight (blue purple) and Tango (coral).

Skinny Singles by Hedgehog Fibres
100% Merino Wool; 400 yds [366 m] / 100 g. Special colorway Anemone.

Merino Singles by La Bien Aimée
100% Merino; 100g; 400 yds [366 m] / 100 g. Special colorway Glacier.

Luxe Light by Walk Collection
70% alpaca, 20% silk, 10% cashmere; 656 yds [600 m] / 100 g. Special colorway Out of the Dark.

Tosh DK by Madelinetosh
100% Merino; 225 yds [206 m] / skein. Special colorway Pebble.

Everyday Sport by The Uncommon Thread
100% Superwash Merino Wool; 330 yds [300 m] / 100 g. Special colorway Spektor.

thank you

Aimee
Akshata
Amy
Beata
Carla
Cathrin
Ce
Charly
Flor
Heather
Iisakki
Jenica
Julie
Karida
Kate
Kristen
Rafa
Sarah &
Hayley
Tiina
Tuulia
Victoria
Virginia

And all our testers. None of this would be possible without you!